ERITREA
A COLONY IN TRANSITION
1941-52

The Royal Institute of International Affairs is an unofficial and non-political body, founded in 1920 to encourage and facilitate the scientific study of international questions. The Institute, as such, is precluded by the terms of its Royal Charter from expressing an opinion on any aspect of international affairs. Any opinions expressed in this publication are not, therefore, those of the Institute.

ERITREA

A COLONY IN TRANSITION: 1941–52

By

G. K. N. TREVASKIS

Issued under the auspices of the
Royal Institute of International Affairs

GREENWOOD PRESS, PUBLISHERS
WESTPORT, CONNECTICUT

Library of Congress Cataloging in Publication Data

Trevaskis, Sir Gerald Kennedy Nicholas, 1915-
    Eritrea : a colony in transition, 1941-52.

    Reprint of the ed. published by Oxford University
Press, London.
    Includes index.
    1. Eritrea--History. I. Title.
[DT395.T7 1975]   963'.5'06   75-3744
ISBN 0-8371-8059-7

© *Royal Institute of International Affairs 1960*

Originally published in 1960 by Oxford University Press,
London, New York

This reprint has been authorized by the Oxford University Press

Reprinted in 1975 by Greenwood Press,
a division of Williamhouse-Regency Inc.

Library of Congress Catalog Card Number 75-3744

ISBN 0-8371-8059-7

Printed in the United States of America

CONTENTS

PREFACE vii

I. THE COUNTRY, ITS HISTORY, AND ITS
   PEOPLE 1
   The Country 1
   The Historical Background 4
   The People 11

II. THE BRITISH IMPACT ON ERITREA,
    1941–50 18
    The Transition from Italian to British Rule 18
    The System of Government 24
    Social and Political Development 29
    Economic Development 36
    Finance 43

III. THE GROWTH OF POLITICAL CONSCIOUSNESS, 1941–7 46
     Urban Xenophobia 46
     Rural Discontent 52
     Ethiopian Nationalism 57
     The Moslem Movement 69
     Italian Intervention 76

IV. THE DISPOSAL OF ERITREA 81
    The Problem 81
    The Failure of the Four Powers to Resolve the
       Problem 83
    The Disposal of Eritrea by the United Nations 92

V. THE TRANSITION TO AUTONOMY IN
   PARTNERSHIP WITH ETHIOPIA, 1951–2 103
   The Problem of Security 103
   The Constitutional Problem 113
   The Transfer of Power 121
   Ethiopia and Eritrea 128

APPENDIX 132
   Population of Eritrea: Communal and Religious
      Groupings 132

Contents

INDEX   134

MAPS
    North East Africa   x
    Eritrea: Physical Regions   2
    Eritrea: Social Groups   12
    Eritrea: Administrative Divisions   20

PREFACE

Until recently the north-eastern corner of Africa was a remote and little known region. Italians, British, and French gained no more than a foothold on its periphery in Eritrea and the Somalilands towards the end of the nineteenth century; Ethiopia withstood European pressure until her conquest by Fascist Italy in 1935. Since the war new and potent forces have been at work. Under the leadership of her Emperor, Ethiopia has emerged as a power of importance on the African and Middle Eastern scene; Eritrea is no longer a colony but an 'autonomous state federated with Ethiopia under the sovereignty of the Ethiopian Crown'; Somalia is to become an independent state in 1960; in British and French Somaliland the throb of nationalism is growing louder. With West Africa, North East Africa is now in the van of African progress. It is better known than it was; it is no longer detached from its neighbours and the rest of the world; it has a leading part to play in the Africa and, perhaps, the Middle East of the future.

This gives Eritrea a peculiar claim to interest. The history of its occupation by the British from April 1941 until September 1952 merits particular attention. It was a period of rapid transition from the narrow colonialism of Fascist Italian rule to quasi-independence within the Ethiopian Federation. It was a period when the country was struck by capricious problems of war and peace; when its inhabitants were caught up in a sudden and deeply disturbing process of revolution; when it came under the shadow of violent disorder and near disruption; and when, for a fleeting moment, it captured the attention of the world. It was a formative period which is likely to leave its mark on Eritrea and its neighbours.

In the history of the British Occupation of Eritrea which follows, I have endeavoured to record what took place during this brief period. I was brought there from British Somaliland as a prisoner of war towards the end of 1940. On my release I was seconded to the British Administration of Eritrea and remained in its service until the summer of 1950, two years before the end of the Occupation. During my time in Eritrea I had the good fortune to serve in most of its districts and, also, to be closely connected with two international commissions which came to conduct inquiries affecting its disposal. Accordingly, I was favourably placed to observe the history of the Occupation unfold itself. My record of it is mainly derived from my own observations, personal correspondence, and official documents and reports which came my way.

Preface

Of the many friends and colleagues upon whom I drew for information were the late Dr. S. F. Nadel, a distinguished anthropologist, who during a brief residence in the country found time to complete a study of Eritrean society and land tenure; Mr. D. Duncanson and the late Mr. B. W. Lee, who took unusual pains to inquire into local history, custom, and sociology and to record what they found; and Messrs. J. T. Crawford, A. C. Jamieson, and J. A. E. Morley who, as administrative officers, were perhaps more closely acquainted with the inhabitants of the country and their problems than most of their colleagues. My notes and records owe much to their industrious researches and shrewd observation.

I owe also a special debt of gratitude to Brigadier S. H. Longrigg and Mr. F. E. Stafford. Brigadier Longrigg, who was head of the British Administration in Eritrea during a critical period at the beginning of the Occupation, has given me generous encouragement and help. To Mr. F. E. Stafford I owe unfailing kindly advice and much of the information covering the last two years of the Occupation after I had left the territory.

G. K. N. TREVASKIS

Aden
1 March 1960

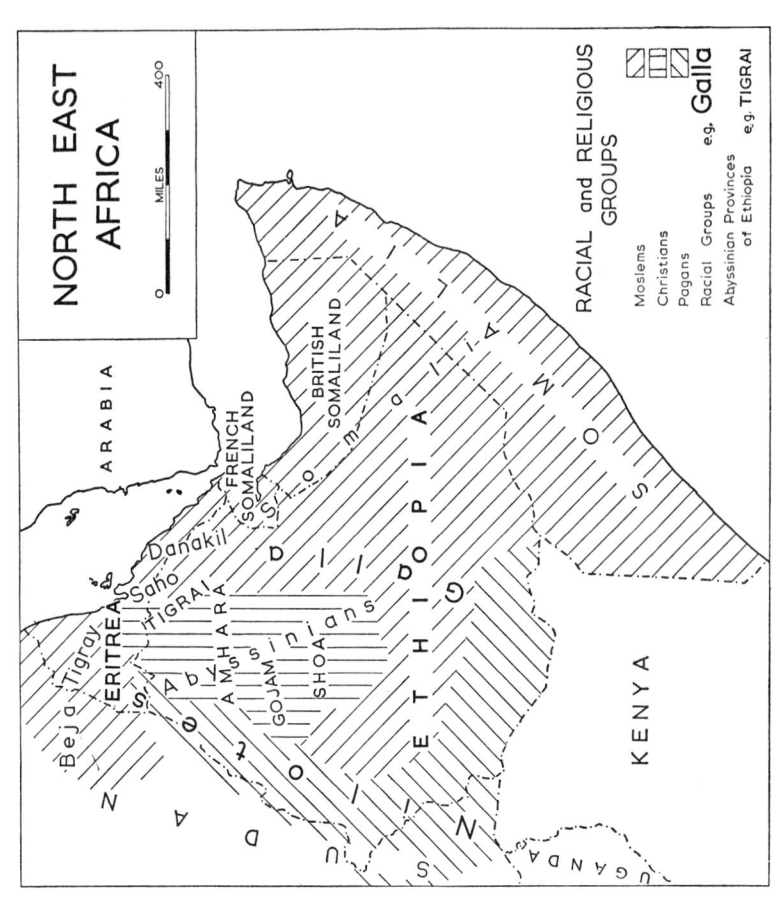

I
THE COUNTRY, ITS HISTORY, AND ITS PEOPLE

The Country

Eritrea lies on the west coast of the Red Sea: a crude triangle wedged untidily between Ethiopia, the Sudan, and French Somaliland. In a continent where the traveller is accustomed to the same deserts stretching unrelieved from horizon to horizon; the same forests or savannah scrub covering vast vegetated areas of monotonous uniformity; and the same lakes, swamps, and marshes extending blankly for mile upon mile—Eritrea's small land surface of barely 50,000 square miles offers a splendid and, perhaps, unique variety. Within it there are compressed microcosms of the Ethiopian highlands, the deserts of the northern Sudan, the 'bush' country of Equatorial Africa, and the severe volcanic wilderness of the South Arabian coast.

The core of the territory is composed of a plateau of thin-soiled moorland decorated with occasional eminences of bare rock and intersected by shallow and, in some cases, fertile valleys and a few deep clefts; this is the northernmost tip of the Ethiopian highlands, with which, at altitudes of 6,000–8,000 feet above sea-level, the Eritrean Plateau shares an agreeable climate, likened by an early English traveller to that of an 'everlasting spring'. Vegetation, mostly in the form of *Euphorbia candelabra*, juniper, and wild olive, is generally sparse, though the Bahri, as the eastern flanks of the plateau are called, are well wooded and a certain amount of scrub is to be found in the Hasamo plain, a curious and comparatively fertile depression lying on its southern border. The plateau drains eastwards into a coastal plain and thence the Red Sea, and westwards into lowlands which reach out into the Sudan. The largest rivers or seasonal watercourses are the Mareb (known in the lowlands as the Gash), the Baraka, and the Anseba, which all flow into the Sudan. The Komaile, Haddas, and Aligede, the larger of the watercourses to flow into the Red Sea, are comparatively small.

From the Plateau a narrowing range of arid but splendidly stark mountains—Eritrea's Northern Highlands—thrusts out northwards across the Sudan frontier. Such poor vegetation as they afford is mainly to be found in the narrow intramontane valleys which twist

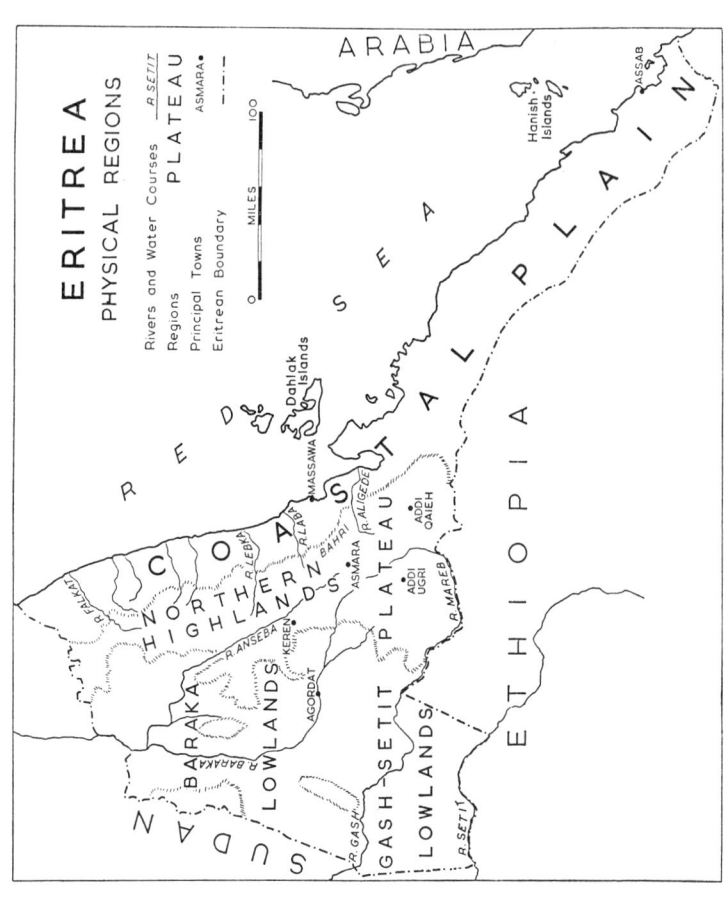

The Country, its History, and its People

and turn between the sterile mountains. In the latter there remain a few unexpected patches of fertility: small plateaus or *rora*, as they are locally known, which lie dispersed about the mountain tops some 6,000–8,000 feet above sea-level and some 3,000–4,000 feet above the valleys below. Conditions in the *rora* resemble those in the Plateau; in the lower-lying valleys the climate is dry and hot and vegetation consists mostly of the acacia varieties. The Northern Highlands form a watershed draining westwards into the Baraka and eastwards into the coastal plain, mainly by way of watercourses known as the Lebka, Laba, and Falkat.

On their immediate west the Plateau and Northern Highlands tumble down some 5,000–6,000 feet into a desert plain which extends into the northern Sudan. This arid expanse of prairie is shot through with sere tinges of life by the turbulent waters of the Baraka and its tributaries, which flow seasonally with a rich cargo of highland silt to the cotton cultivations of Tokar in the Sudan. The banks of the Baraka and its satellites support a pleasing forest of dom palms; elsewhere, away from these narrow ribbons of fertility, there is nothing to relieve the tedium of sand and gravel but meagre growths of stunted acacia.

To the south-east of the Baraka Lowlands the countryside changes with surprising abruptness from desert to what might, if euphemistically, be termed forest. Here between the rivers Gash and Setit (or Takazze, as it is known in Ethiopia) the soils are rich and black; vegetation is thick and, during the rains, the grass is lush and plentiful. These hot, humid, and consequently malarial lowlands dotted thickly with a rash of varied acacias extend southwards and westwards into western Ethiopia and the southern provinces of the Sudan.

On the east the Plateau and Northern Highlands descend sharply and spectacularly into a coastal plain which fringes the Red Sea; sandy and narrow in the north and increasingly extensive in the south where it expands into the volcanic waste of north-eastern Ethiopia and French Somaliland. The climate is intensely hot and humid in the summer and, save for a few narrow belts of rich alluvial deposits by the beds of the major watercourses, the country is an inhospitable desert of sand, gravel, and volcanic rock relieved only in the more favoured parts by sparse and scattered mimosa shrubs.

In a territory of such physical variety it is not surprising that rainfall should vary both in degree and seasonal incidence as between the different regions. There are two well-defined seasons. From June to September the 'summer rains' fall in all parts of the territory other than the Coastal Plain; from November to January the 'winter rains' fall in the Coastal Plain, though seldom in its southern extre-

Eritrea

mity. In addition the regions covered by the 'summer rains' usually enjoy a few showers during April. Rainfall is generally heaviest in the south. As much as 20–25 inches may be expected on the Plateau and in the Gash-Setit Lowlands. It diminishes farther to the north, rainfall in the Northern Highlands and Baraka Lowlands averaging from seven to ten inches and, in the northern stretch of the Coastal Plain, about four inches. The Bahri, because of its favoured position on the eastern flanks of the Plateau, benefits both from summer and winter rains and enjoys a rainfall of forty or more inches in a year.

The Historical Background

Eritrea was created, and so named, by the Italians, who established their first colony towards the end of the nineteenth century in this small sliver of territory on the western shores of the Red or 'Erythrean' Sea. Before this Eritrea had never enjoyed any form of unity, had never had a government of its own, had never even had a name. It was characteristic of contemporary colonial ventures that Italy's first colony should have been determined solely by the military capacity of its Italian invaders. No concession was made to physical geography, past history, or the racial and cultural complexion of its inhabitants.

'Eritrea's' earliest inhabitants are believed to have been a Nilotic people, negroid forest dwellers, who had moved from their homes in the thick bush of the south-eastern Sudan into the Gash-Setit Lowlands and thence to the Plateau. Later 'Eritrea' was invaded by pastoral Hamitic tribes, who swept down from the deserts of the Northern Sudan, occupied the Baraka Lowlands and Northern Highlands, subjugating or expelling their Nilotic inhabitants and spreading along the barren coastal desert into the lowlands of north-eastern Ethiopia and the Somalilands. They were followed by 'Sabaeans', Semites who crossed the Red Sea to colonize the Plateau, where the climate and countryside closely resembled the South Arabian highlands from which they had come. The newcomers brought with them some knowledge of political organization and agricultural techniques: also they had experience in commerce and boasted contacts with the civilized world which would enable them to turn it to account.

Little is known of these early 'Eritreans' until the emergence of a kingdom centred on Axum, which lies within Ethiopia close to the Eritrean Plateau, during the first century of the Christian era. Within it the half-caste communities of Sabaean and Hamitic stock who had developed on the Plateau, and who, because of their hybrid ancestry, later acquired the name of Habash or 'mixed' (from which

The Country, its History, and its People

is derived the term 'Abyssinian'), were dominant. Their power stemmed from the Sabaeans' comparative political maturity and the wealth which they were able to generate from the trade flowing through the port of Adulis (the modern Zula) from and to Egypt and the countries of the Eastern Mediterranean, Red Sea, and Persian Gulf. Though the first Axumite kings affected a Greek culture, derived from Graeco-Roman Egypt, and employed Greek as their official language, the Axumites or early Abyssinians remained for the most part wedded to the Semitic culture of their Sabaean ancestors. In the event, the subsequent arrival of a fresh wave of South Arabian immigrants, the Himyarites, firmly established a Semitic culture amongst the Plateau communities and, with it, the classical Ethiopic language of Ge'ez.

Axum attained its greatest power from the fourth to the sixth centuries. The ruins of temples, baths, and towns, which may still be seen dispersed along the route between Axum and Zula, bear witness to the presence on the Plateau at this time of an ordered society which demanded and secured a higher standard of living than any 'Eritreans' or indeed 'Ethiopians' were to enjoy until recently. Though Axumite civilization was largely restricted to the Plateau, the Hamitic tribes came under direct Axumite influence and control, as a consequence of which the less remote abandoned their harsh Hamitic dialects for the soft Semitic Ge'ez of their Axumite rulers. From a region which was approximately coextensive with modern Eritrea and formed the core of their empire, the Christian kings of Axum extended their power and influence far afield. Their armies marched westwards into Nubia to conquer and destroy the kingdom of Meroe: at the request of the Emperor Justinian, they even crossed the Red Sea to subjugate the whole of Arabia Felix on the pretext of preserving the Christians of South Arabia from Jewish persecution.

After the sixth century their power declined as a direct consequence of the Arab invasion of Egypt. Its effect was to force the Hamitic, and mainly Beja, tribes of eastern Egypt and the northern Sudan southwards and, thereby, to project their Beja kinsmen already in the Northern Highlands and Baraka Lowlands on to the Plateau. Axumite civilization crumbled under the invasion of the barbarians. Cut off from the sea by a wedge of lawless tribesmen, Axum was cut off also from the commerce upon which its prosperity and power had been founded. Thus the early Abyssinians of Axum were forced to expand southwards, withdrawing into an obscurity from which they were only to emerge some seven centuries later as the dominant element of the early Abyssinian or Ethiopian empire.

Eritrea

'Eritrea' was abandoned to anarchy. The Plateau, Northern Highlands, and Baraka Lowlands were given over to the Beja; the Danakil, another Hamitic people, occupied the remote and inhospitable maritime desert of Eritrea's southern extremity; and the small groups of Nilotes continued to shelter in the disagreeable and uncoveted forests of the Gash-Setit Lowlands.

There was little change in the texture of Eritrean society until the Plateau was invaded by immigrants from the Ethiopian interior during the fourteenth and fifteenth centuries. The first wave was composed of 'Agau from Lasta, a people of Hamitic origin who had, however, set up the Zagwe dynasty, which had ruled in Ethiopia from shortly after the fall of Axum until the restoration of the Solomonian dynasty in 1270. They were followed by groups of Abyssinians from Dambeya and the Tigrai who, with the 'Agau, wrested the Plateau from the Beja; either subjugating them or expelling them into the Northern Highlands and the Baraka Lowlands. After an interruption of several centuries the Plateau had once more become an outpost of Abyssinian culture and Ethiopian political power. The Abyssinians raided into the lowlands but never remained to garrison them; they plundered but never governed. And though the less disagreeable climate of the Northern Highlands attracted small expeditions of Abyssinian colonists, they tended to become assimilated to the nomadic folk among whom they lived. Their own Abyssinian culture became diluted with Beja strains; their Coptic churches crumbled into ruins; they retained nothing of their Abyssinian past but their names and genealogies.

The failure of Ethiopia's Abyssinian vanguard to control the beduin tribes encircling the Plateau was to prove costly. By permitting vacua to persist around her northern outposts Ethiopia invited alien intrusion. The process began during the sixteenth century, a time when Christian Ethiopia was engaged in a bitter and seemingly hopeless struggle with the Moslems of the Somali Coast. In 1557 the Turks established themselves at Massawa and acquired some form of control over the northern stretch of the Coastal Plain. During the same century the Fung, half-caste, negroid Arabs who had established a kingdom in the central Sudan towards the end of the fifteenth century, expanded eastwards gaining influence, if not always control, over the Gash-Setit and Baraka Lowlands. At the same time the Danakil and other Hamitic tribes of north-eastern Ethiopia were welded into a loose unity by the Anfari or Sultans of Aussa, dependants of the Somali kings of Adal. The shape of Eritrea's partition between Ethiopians, Turks, Fung, and the Sultans of Aussa, though fluid at first, congealed into a recognizable shape.

The Country, its History, and its People

It thawed out in the warmth of the imperialistic sun which dawned over Africa during the nineteenth century. The first of the new imperialists were the Egyptians who invaded the northern Sudan in the earlier part of the century and, as the political successors of the Fung, later extended their authority to the Baraka Lowlands. But success and conquest served rather to stimulate Egyptian appetites than otherwise. With the opening of the Suez Canal in 1869 the Red Sea, so long a remote backwater, emerged as one of the world's principal maritime routes. The north-eastern corner of Africa was no longer a remote asylum of picturesque barbarism but a potential market and source of riches and power. The Egyptians swiftly established themselves along the Red Sea and Somali coasts, hemming in north and eastern Ethiopia with an impressive green fringe which appeared on maps of that time. By 1872 the process was complete. In Eritrea the Egyptian flag had been hoisted in place of the Turkish at Massawa and Egyptian authority had been extended to the coastal clans. The Lowlands of the Baraka and Gash-Setit were Egyptian, and Egyptian troops were garrisoning Keren, the key to the Northern Highlands.

Keren was also the gateway to the Plateau and the distant highlands of Ethiopia. Thus the Egyptians were now well poised for the invasion and conquest of unconquered Ethiopia. Their decision to advance was largely influenced by Werner Munzinger, a Swiss in Egyptian employment and a recognized expert on north Ethiopian affairs. Munzinger's belief that Ethiopia would be unable to resist an invasion largely derived from his personal experience as political adviser to the Napier Expedition. Lord Napier's troops had entered Ethiopia in 1867 and had defeated the Emperor Theodore in April 1868 with barely the loss of a man. The victory, though military in form, had been political in character and had been gained through the defection of John, the ruler of the Ethiopian province of the Tigrai and, since Theodore's death, Emperor of Ethiopia. In Munzinger's view Ethiopia could always be conquered by skilful exploitation of her endemic dynastic feuds and the use of well-equipped troops. The Egyptians advanced into the Plateau in 1875 under the leadership of an American chief of staff. They were defeated at Gundet in the same year and were finally routed at Gura in 1876. Munzinger had viewed Ethiopian patriotism too cynically. John assisted Napier to win the throne for himself; he would never have betrayed Theodore if he had believed that the British intended to occupy Ethiopia. Thus, contrary to Munzinger's calculations, there was no rift in the Ethiopian ranks; Egyptian pretensions lent the Emperor John the support of a united people and with it he threw

Eritrea

out the invader. The Egyptians withdrew from the Plateau but, thanks to General Gordon's diplomacy, remained in possession of the Eritrean provinces which they had previously occupied.

Their further enjoyment of them was swiftly and decisively terminated by the outbreak of the Mahdist revolt. By 1882 the Egyptian garrisons in Eritrea found themselves uncomfortably sandwiched between the Mahdists, who were then in complete control of the northern Sudan, and the hostile Abyssinians of the Emperor John's army. They could not hold their positions; they could neither withdraw nor advance; they were trapped. They were saved from their awkward predicament by British intervention, as a result of which the Emperor John agreed both to give the Egyptians safeconduct to their troopships at Massawa and to assist in the suppression of the Mahdist revolt. The Emperor loyally adhered to his side of the bargain. Five Egyptian garrisons were rescued; the Mahdists were heavily defeated by the Abyssinians at Kufit and Metemma (where the Emperor lost his life in the fighting); and, by containing an appreciable part of the Mahdist forces, the Abyssinians relieved the pressure on the British and Egyptians operating in the north.

These services were poorly rewarded. The Emperor had understood that, in return for his help, the British would use their influence to enable him to acquire Massawa and Keren so that he might then extend his authority to the Northern Highlands and the Coastal Plain. As it was, the Italians, who had been established at Assab on the Danakil coast since 1882, occupied Massawa in 1885; a move which was connived at and, indeed, encouraged by the British, who saw in the development of Italian influence in the Red Sea a useful counter to the French, who were by this time seated at Djibouti. The Italians lost no time in bringing the coastal tribes under their protection and, by lending covert assistance to Menelik, John's rival for the throne, in preparing to extend their influence into the Ethiopian interior. Their initial efforts to advance were successfully resisted by John's troops, though, because of Ethiopian undertakings to the British, they were also fighting against the Mahdists in the west. But, with John's death at Metemma in 1889, Menelik quickly seized power and, in return for their help, allowed the Italians to enter the Plateau unopposed. Italy had acquired her first colony, and Eritrea had come into being.

Because they had used Menelik to win the Plateau, the Italians believed that they could continue using him to extend their influence across the rich and undeveloped vastness of Ethiopia. They seemed unaware that Menelik had also made use of them to serve his own purpose and that, having won his prize, he would prove less

The Country, its History, and its People

malleable than when, as an aspirant to the imperial throne, he had sought their help. In the event he soon dispelled any illusions that he was prepared to be an Italian puppet. By the Treaty of Uccialli, which Menelik and the Italians signed in 1889, the latter understood Ethiopia to have accepted Italian protection and with it to have renounced her right to conduct relations with foreign powers except through the Italian Government. Menelik argued that he was required to do no more than inform the protecting power of his correspondence with foreign governments. It was a question of words in different languages and their interpretation. The Italians understood one thing; Menelik another. By subsequently entering into direct negotiations with the Russians and the French, the Emperor left the Italians in no doubt that he had the determination to suit his action to his arguments.

It was at this stage that the Italians blundered as the Egyptians had blundered before them. Believing Menelik to have betrayed them, they decided to abandon him and transfer their patronage to a more pliant protégé. In this mood their attention was attracted by the evident hostility of the Tigrinyan population to the Emperor. In the Tigrai there was little love for Menelik, who was not a Tigrinyan, and a good deal of resentment that on the Tigrinyan John's death the imperial crown had passed out of the Tigrai. Moreover Ras Mangasha, the ruler of the Tigrai, was transparently ambitious and seemed ready to intrigue against his Emperor. Italian interference in the Tigrai quickly set the frontier ablaze with incidents which provided the Italians with the opportunity to invade and occupy the greater part of the Tigrai in 1894–5. Italian imperialism was suddenly revealed in an ominous nakedness which shocked Ras Mangasha and his followers into a belated but effective loyalty to Ethiopia and her ruler. In December 1895 the Ethiopians routed the Italians at Amba Alagi, in January 1896 the Italian garrison at Makalle was forced to surrender, and, by February, the Tigrai was cleared of Italian troops. In a desperate and ill-considered attempt to retrieve their position the Italians launched a surprise attack on the Tigrinyan frontier town of Adowa and, there, on 1 March, suffered one of the most humiliating defeats in Italian history. Once again the endemic xenophobia of the Abyssinian had triumphed over his factiousness; once again a foreign invader had failed to understand the latent strength of Abyssinian patriotism.

The memory of Adowa lingered on in Italy long after peace had been made and the frontiers of the colony of Eritrea had received Ethiopian recognition. It kept alive an Italian desire for vengeance which, in the political and economic climate of Fascism in the 1930's,

Eritrea

suddenly flared up into a lust for power and imperial possessions in backward and weak Ethiopia. The Italian invasion and conquest of Ethiopia in 1935–6 were succeeded in 1936 by the union of Ethiopia, Eritrea, and Somalia in the Italian East African Empire. This was the culmination of Italian achievement and had no precedent in history. Italy had both created Eritrea and united it effectively with Ethiopia and the greater part of the Somali territories.

Today it has become fashionable to deride what is contemptuously referred to as 'Western colonialism', as though colonial rule were nothing more than crude exploitation of a subject people for the enrichment of their alien rulers. In the context of the modern world, where the cliché that good government is no substitute for self-government is now widely accepted, partial judgements of this kind meet with readier credence than any apologists for colonial rule. The objective student however would do well to take account of local conditions at the time when colonial rule was first established in a territory and to consider what the lot of its inhabitants would have been had it not experienced alien government. He would do well also to compare present-day conditions in backward countries such as Yemen and Saudi Arabia which have never suffered colonial rule with those in their sister Arab countries which have. The colonial governments, he will find, have made mistakes; they may often have acted selfishly; but few will have given nothing in return.

This is particularly true in the case of the Italian régime in Eritrea. Its policy was, as we shall see, in some respects cynical and selfish, but at the same time it brought the Eritrean people benefits which their forefathers had never known, and which they themselves would not otherwise have enjoyed. Peace was introduced to lend value to human life long cheapened by personal and tribal vendettas; the impartial justice of the law courts was brought to a people accustomed to the prevalence of the strong over the weak; slavery, which had hung like a black cloud over the primitive negroid inhabitants of the Gash-Setit, was dispelled; the pestilences and diseases which had repeatedly wiped out thousands of head of animals at a time and had decimated families and clans were brought under control; famine became a memory to those who had lived in a constant fear of it; and the people grew fat and contented in the unfamiliar warmth of civilized government.

In all this Italians may justly take pride. But in conceding Italy's contribution to human happiness in this small country the real significance of the Italian régime in Eritrea must not be overlooked. Italy created Eritrea by an act of surgery: by severing its different

The Country, its History, and its People

peoples from those with whom their past had been linked and by grafting the amputated remnants to each other under the title of Eritrean.

THE PEOPLE

The capricious manner of Eritrea's creation, its long history of immigrations, invasions, and partition between alien rulers, and the physical diversity of its terrain have left their stamp on the inhabitants. They are not in any accepted sense a single people but a conglomerate of different communities which are themselves in most cases akin by culture and blood to their neighbours in Ethiopia, the Sudan, and French Somaliland.

The largest of these communities inhabits the Plateau and is an offshoot of the Abyssinian people inhabiting the Tigrai.[1] Of a Tigrinyan population of some 1,500,000 about 524,000 live in Eritrea. Like their Ethiopian kinsmen the great majority are Coptic Christians. In all there are 487,000 Christians[2] as against only 37,000 Moslems.

Tigrinyan society in Eritrea broadly subdivides into one group of families which claims descent from a mythical common ancestor named Meroni through three sons with the quaint names Faluk, Chaluk, and Maluk, and another which derives from early 'Agau clans collectively named the Adkameh Malaga. The former live with the families associated with them in the Hamasain and Akelli Guzai districts of the Plateau: the latter in the district of Serai.

The Tigrinyans are settled agriculturists and are organized in village communities which are each composed of varying numbers of extended families. Most of these families are the original occupants and, therefore, owners of the land. They are known as *restenya*, while the families which immigrated later and are their tenants are the *makalai ailet*. Both classes of family enjoy the same rights of user in the land but only the *restenya* have a right to a voice in the management of the village. Domestically it is administered by committees of elders representing the *restenya* families: governmentally it is in the charge of a headman or *chiqa* who by tradition is invariably appointed from a particular family of *restenya*.

For administrative purposes the Plateau districts subdivide into a large number of sub-districts which in the past were variously administered on behalf of the Ethiopian Emperors by officers known as *faresainya* and hereditary chiefs[3] or left to fend for themselves. The

---
[1] The term 'Abyssinian' is used to describe the dominant racial group in Ethiopia, which inhabits the provinces of Amhara, Tigrai, Gojam, and Shoa.
[2] See Appendix, p. 132, below.
[3] These chiefs were usually known as *shumanya*. There were also *shum gulti* who held fiefs from the Emperor

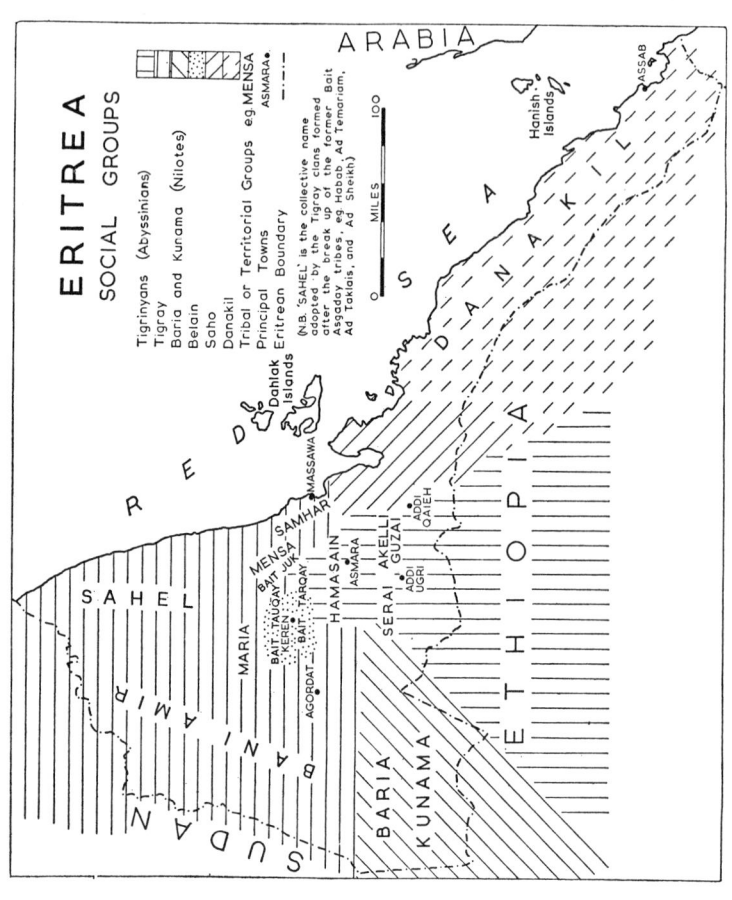

The Country, its History, and its People

Italians introduced uniformity by putting chiefs in charge of all subdistricts and appointing their own nominees, who were not always chosen from the traditional chiefly families. Similarly they appointed their own nominees to village headmanships, often ignoring the rights of the families from which the appointments were traditionally made.

Their common Ethiopic dialect of Tigrinya, their Abyssinian culture, and, perhaps, above all the loyalty of the overwhelming majority of Tigrinyans to the Coptic Church both provide a cultural solidarity as between Ethiopian and Eritrean Tigrinyans and culturally link them closely with the other Abyssinian peoples of Ethiopia. The influence of the Coptic Church over the lives and behaviour of the Eritrean Tigrinyans cannot be overstated. In Eritrea, which for ecclesiastical purposes is included in the diocese of the Abuna or Bishop of the Tigrai, as many as twenty or thirty priests, deacons, and acolytes minister to the spiritual needs of each village and, scattered about the Plateau and its periphery, several ancient monastic communities of monks and nuns exercise a powerful and reactionary influence in their support.

This to some extent accounts for the severe intolerance of the Christian for the Moslem minority. With few exceptions the Jiberti or 'elect', as the Moslems are known, are denied any rights in land, are treated as social outcasts, and live as traders and craftsmen. Not surprisingly the great majority have today sought refuge in the less intolerant society of the towns.

To their north and west, dispersed along the northern stretch of the Coastal Plain and about the Northern Highlands and Baraka Lowlands, there are tribes which speak Tigray, the closest spoken derivative of the classical Ethiopic Ge'ez. In Eritrea they number 329,000: an additional 23,000 live near-by in the Tokar district of the Sudan. Culturally they are in many respects akin to the Beja 'Fuzzy Wuzzies' of the Sudan whom they mostly resemble in appearance and physique. Like them they are Moslems and adhere to a sect known as the Khatmia,[4] and like them they are mostly pastoral nomads or at least of semi-nomadic habits.[5]

Despite their claims to Arab ancestry most Tigray families are probably the descendants of early Beja, Sabaean, and Himyaritic immigrants. The original clans, however, came under the domina-

[4] Founded by Saiyid Mohammed Uthman al Mirghani who died in the Sudan in 1853.
[5] Many Tigray tribesmen in the Northern Highlands have taken to agriculture during the past fifty years and, though most still migrate seasonally with their herds and flocks, some now remain in semi-permanent encampments near their lands.

Eritrea

tion of families enjoying the support of the Fung kings and Ethiopian emperors during the fifteenth and sixteenth centuries. Thus an Abyssinian clan from the Plateau, the Bait Asgaday, and the Maria and Mensa, Saho clans[6] enjoying Ethiopian patronage, partitioned most of the Northern Highlands while the Bani Amir, a Ja'alin family from the Sudan and protégés of the Fung, assumed control of the Baraka Lowlands.

Within the tribal organizations which emerged as a consequence[7] the dominant families became an aristocratic caste to which their Tigray subjects were obliged to tender a number of exacting dues and services. At the same time the heads of the aristocratic families developed as powerful tribal chiefs. With the advent of the Italians it was natural that the Tigray, who had become no more than serfs, should seek to be freed from their disagreeable obligations. In the event the Italians, while abolishing the more intolerable dues and services owed by the Tigray, found the traditional political and social structure of the tribes too convenient for their purposes to be unduly weakened by reform. And so they were careful to support the authority of the traditional chiefs and, thereby, preserved the obnoxious social system over which they presided.

The southern stretch of the Coastal Plain and the vast desert lying about it in Ethiopia and French Somaliland are thinly inhabited by the Danakil, a Moslem people who speak a Hamitic dialect called Afar, and are culturally akin to the other Eastern Hamites, the Galla and Somalis. In Eritrea there are some 33,000 Danakil; in Ethiopia about 70,000.

The Danakil are organized as small clans or families, which now come under the loose control of a number of petty shaikhs, some of whom have at various times assumed the title of Sultan, exercising a territorial jurisdiction from the few semi-permanent centres which have developed in this inhospitable country. Traditionally they owe a loose allegiance to the Sultan or Anfari of Aussa (in Ethiopia), which the Italian regime did nothing to weaken.

Between the Danakil and the Tigrinyans, uneasily perched on the eastern edge of the Plateau and scattered about the foothills and plains below, are the Saho. In Eritrea they number 66,000; an additional 40,000 live across the border in Ethiopia. With the exception

[6] See below, pp. 14–15.

[7] The three principal Bait Asgaday families established tribes known as the Habab, Ad Taklais, and Ad Temariam, while an Abyssinian follower of Asgaday's named Gabib Ruk seceded with his family to form another tribe, later named the Bait Juk. The Maria split to form two tribes, the Red and Black Maria and, like them, the Mensa split into the Mensa Bait Shakan and Mensa Bait Ebrahay. The Bani Amir alone preserved their unity.

The Country, its History, and its People

of a negligible minority[8] the Eritrean Saho are Moslems: their kinsmen in Ethiopia are mostly Christians. The majority are pastoral nomads or semi-nomadic. A few on the Plateau are settled agriculturists.

The origins of the Saho are obscure but their language, which is a Hamitic dialect closely related to Afar, suggests that they were by origin also Eastern Hamites. By their proximity to the Tigrinyans on the Plateau and the Tigray on the Coastal Plain they have, however, acquired many Abyssinian and Tigray customs and practices which today predominate over those which they share with the Danakil. In appearance most tend to resemble the Tigray.

The Saho are organized as clans which have become federated into five tribes, Assa'orta, Hazu, Minaferi, Debrimaila and Sana'fay. Before the Italian régime they had no chiefs, their affairs being managed in a haphazard fashion by councils of elders. This did not suit the Italians' need for close control and accordingly they appointed chiefs in charge of each tribe: a measure which made for administrative efficiency if not for popularity.

Lying in the shadow of the Plateau at the southern end of the Northern Highlands is a region known as Bogus. Its centre is the town of Keren and it is the country of the Belain. They number about 38,000 of whom 27,000 are Moslems and 11,000 Christians.[9]

The Belain are composed of a number of small families mostly of Abyssinian or Tigray origins which came under the control of two powerful clans—the Bait Tarqay and Bait Tauqay—during the sixteenth century. The Bait Tarqay were Hamites and immigrants from 'Agau in Ethiopia; the Bait Tauqay were Tigrinyans from the Plateau. The Bait Tarqay brought with them the Hamitic dialect used in 'Agau, which they subsequently passed on to the Bait Tauqay and which has since developed as a distinctive dialect.

Within the two tribal organizations the members of the dominant class are known as *simager* and those of the subject families as *mikiru*. The relationship between them resembles that between the Tigrinyan *restenya* and *makalai ailet*. Before the arrival of the Italians the *sims* or heads of the families into which the Bait Tarqay and Bait Tauqay subdivided exercised a chiefly authority over their own families and the *mikiru* attached to them. There were, however, no chiefs with authority over the whole of either of the tribes and, as in the case of the Saho, their affairs were loosely managed by councils of elders until the Italians appointed paramount chiefs over each of the two tribes in 1932.

Though they share a common language and many common cus-

[8] See Appendix, p. 133, below.   [9] Ibid.

Eritrea

toms, the two tribes have tended to grow culturally apart. The Bait Tarqay, who are the immediate neighbours of the Tigrinyans, are mostly Christians and, though many are still semi-nomadic, many are becoming settled agriculturists and some are beginning to live in villages similar to those on the Plateau. At the same time, intermarriage and contact with the Tigrinyans has resulted in their adopting Abyssinian customs and inclining towards an Abyssinian culture. As against this the Bait Tauqay, who are all Moslems and mostly lead a nomadic or semi-nomadic life, are becoming culturally assimilated to the neighbouring Tigray.

And finally, in the remote lowlands of the Gash-Setit, there are the Baria and Kunama, offshoots of the Nilotic peoples inhabiting western Ethiopia and the Southern Sudan. They speak closely related Nilotic dialects, are settled agriculturists, and number about 41,000. In the past they were all pagans. Today about 3,000 are converts to Christianity, about 31,000 profess to be Moslems, and the remainder continue as pagans to worship their ancestors and to believe in a variety of spirits.[10]

Though there are still traces of earlier exogamic totem clans amongst the Kunama, today they and the Baria are organized on a territorial basis, living in villages which are regionally grouped into what they themselves call 'tribes'. There is, however, a significant difference in their social structure. Among the Kunama descent is matrilineal: amongst the Baria it is patrilineal, as elsewhere in Eritrea. Because of this the Baria have been able to retain an earlier clan and family organization, which persists in their present village communities. In the Kunama villages there is no comparable family organization.

Traditionally the affairs of the Baria and Kunama were managed by occasional meetings of elders and, though leaders sometimes emerged, nothing approximating to chieftainship was known until the Egyptians appointed a prominent Baria named Totil to collect taxes and execute their orders. The Italians improved on Egyptian practice by converting the position held by Totil into a hereditary chieftainship extending to the Kunama as well as to the Baria.

This measure was deeply resented by the Kunama who are now culturally very much less close to the Baria than they once were. The Kunama remain predominantly Nilotic and, whatever religions some may now profess, they are mostly wedded to their pagan traditions. The Baria are now all Moslems and have largely become assimilated to their Tigray neighbours, whose customs they have in many respects adopted.

[10] See Appendix, p. 132, below.

The Country, its History, and its People

And so Eritrea is inhabited by a curious mosaic of diverse communities. They have various origins; all have links with other communities across Eritrea's borders. Some are Christian; others Moslem; a few professedly pagan. Some are settled agriculturists; others in varying degrees live as pastoral nomads. They have little in common with each other but the accident of their residence in the territory Italy conquered and named Eritrea.

II

THE BRITISH IMPACT ON ERITREA
1941-50

The Transition from Italian to British Rule

Within a year of Italy's making war on Britain Mussolini's East African Empire dissolved in the shambles of swift and humiliating defeat. Italy declared war on 10 June 1940; by May 1941 British forces had occupied Eritrea, Italian Somaliland, and all of Ethiopia except the remote and isolated eminence of Gondar, where what was left of the Duke of Aosta's[1] army was to put up its last dispirited stand. After a rapid advance across the lowland plains of the Baraka the British forces entering Eritrea from the Sudan had been halted before the impressive mountain wall guarding Keren, the key to the Eritrean Plateau, and Asmara, the territory's capital city. With the arrival of reinforcements the advance continued, the heights of Keren were stormed after the first and only battle of the campaign, and, on 1 April 1941, British troops entered Asmara. By 8 April, with the fall of the Red Sea port of Massawa, the whole of Eritrea was in British occupation: four days after the British commander, General (later Sir William) Platt, had installed himself in the stucco palace of the former Italian Governor at Asmara.

Though waged on a comparatively small scale, war had produced its familiar crop of confusion and human suffering. Asmara and the larger towns were crammed with Italian civilian refugees and fugitive soldiery mostly out of uniform. The countryside was scoured by hungry, desperate, and armed native soldiers, from Somalia and Ethiopia, who had been left to find their way home as best they could. Italian civil authority had ceased to function; and, with the British as yet ill prepared to take on civil responsibilities, there was a serious threat of widespread disorder. Stocks of food, already wasted by the improvidence of Italian officialdom, were dangerously low. Italian defeat had brought Eritrea into the shadows of disease, disorder, and famine.

Though shocked by defeat, the Italians had not lost heart. British victory was not the sign for Italian disillusionment about Mussolini's war or for more than a few furtive recantations of former Fascist

---

[1] Viceroy of Italian East Africa. He subsequently died as a prisoner of war in Kenya.

The British Impact on Eritrea, 1941-50

loyalties. Most Italians welcomed the end of local hostilities but remained as receptive as ever to the propaganda of their Fascist leaders, who claimed that, though Italian East Africa was temporarily lost, Britain would still lose the war. In Eritrea the more optimistic predicted British defeat before the close of the year: few believed that the Axis would not regain Eritrea after the summer rains. A campaign might have been lost but victory was still in prospect.

Nor did British victory immediately win over the Eritreans to the British cause. They had been imbued with a deep, if unthinking, loyalty to their Italian rulers. Many had served in the Army until final defeat, and, throughout the campaign, the civilian population had remained unquestioningly obedient to Italian authority. They were now disassociated from their old rulers but, as yet, had no links with or affection for the British. In the main the change of authority did not trouble them with problems of loyalty. For most, it had a very different meaning. Memories of previous changes of authority were not dead. It was at the time of the Egyptian occupation and withdrawal, and when Italy had seized Eritrea, that disputed boundaries had been changed, old scores paid off, and chieftainships transferred from one family to another. In some cases there had been a resort to force; in most those who had gained by the changes of régime had done so by favour of the incoming authority. And so Italian defeat left the Eritrean thinking of rights to be seized or safeguarded and wrongs to be avenged. Everywhere British officers were bombarded with petitions demanding the recovery of land, the reversal of judgements, the deposition or punishment of chiefs and officials. In a few cases Eritreans took the law into their own hands.

By ill chance the British had to undertake this difficult Eritrean commitment at a time of military reverses and embarrassments in the Middle and Near East. On 31 March 1941—the day before the surrender of Asmara—Rommel launched an attack which swept the British out of most of Cyrenaica and left their garrison at Tobruk encircled; in April and May Greece and Crete were overwhelmed; and it was only the prompt suppression of Rashid 'Ali's revolt in Iraq and the hasty invasion of Syria in June that forestalled the occupation of those countries by the Axis. All this could be expected to encourage Italian resistance to British authority in Eritrea and that at a time when the garrison would have to be reduced to meet the urgent demands for reinforcements.

Unfortunately the British were ill prepared for their Eritrean responsibilities. It had been supposed that General Platt would be halted indefinitely before the heights of Keren; and consequently

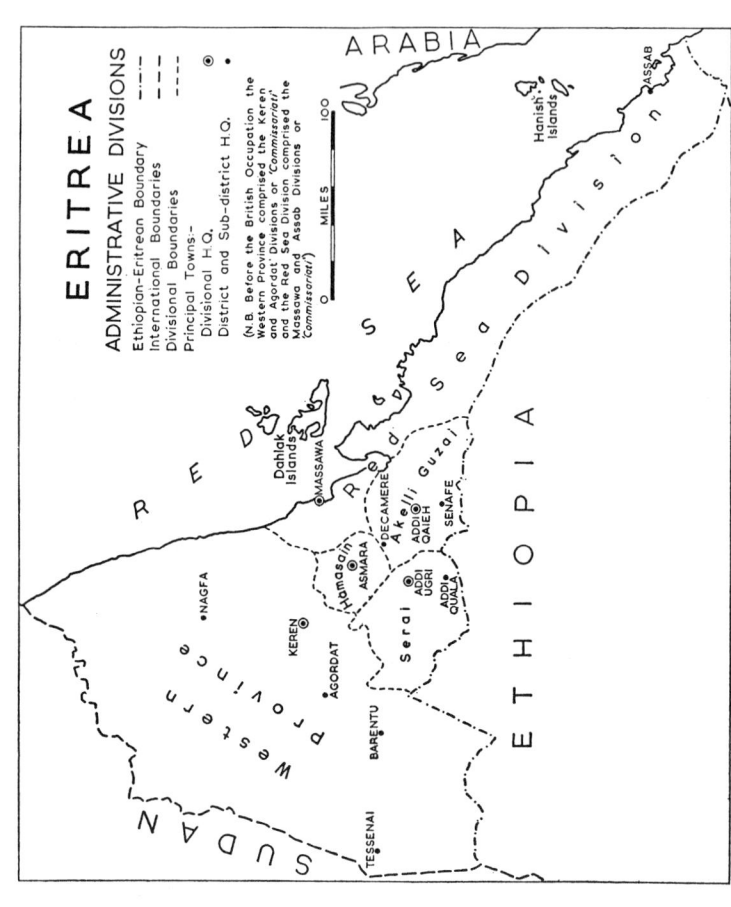

The British Impact on Eritrea, 1941–50

arrangements had only been made for the administration of the Baraka and Gash-Setit Lowlands, which comprised what was then the Agordat administrative division.

This, it was envisaged, would be administered by officers of the Sudan Administration as an appendage of the adjacent Sudan province of Kassala. And so, at the time of his entry into Asmara, General Platt had no more than Brigadier B. Kennedy-Cooke (the former Governor of the Kassala province), eight British officers, and nine Sudanese policemen with whom to take over the civil administration of Eritrea. Though plans were made to recruit additional officers from East Africa and the Middle East it seemed improbable that sufficient would be forthcoming to fill more than a fraction of the senior administrative appointments.

Fortunately, the officials of the Italian Administration remained anxious and expectant at their posts. The only practicable course was to invite them to continue under such British control as could be improvised. This was done, and the former departments of the Italian Administration continued to function much as before, under varying degrees of British supervision and the general control of a hastily created British Secretariat. The only department where urgent steps were taken to bring Italian control to an end was the police. The two Italian organizations—the Royalist *carabinieri* and strongly Fascist *Polizia Africana Italiana*—could scarcely be expected to enjoy British confidence as instruments of security. They were speedily disbanded and replaced by a newly raised police force.

This makeshift arrangement had many shortcomings, but it ensured continuity of government during the dangerous and uneasy period of transition from Italian to British authority. Also the resemblance of the new to the old régime had a usefully sedative effect implying a return to normal. Italian uneasiness was calmed by the sight of a familiar bureaucracy attending to the routine of public business. Similarly a dangerous Eritrean effervescence very soon subsided.

For this the British were largely indebted to the accommodating behaviour of the Italian officials. Had they chosen to leave their posts, not all the troops then moving northwards to help in the defence of Egypt could have been spared. Nevertheless if this Italian collaboration helped the British to establish their authority peacefully, it also rendered them uncomfortably dependent on Italian behaviour and temper. Many Italians had access to secret caches of arms and ammunition, Italian officials held most of the principal executive appointments in the public services, and a number of hotheaded young Fascists were still at large.

Eritrea

In this situation the British had a choice between two alternatives. The need for quick results argued in favour of a policy of ruthless repression to induce swift Italian submission. In its support was the not unreasonable belief that most Italians had been educated through Fascism to respect force. Alternatively, it was arguable that more lasting and effective results would be achieved at less cost if the Italian population were weaned from Fascism by firm but sympathetic treatment. Neither course was free from risk. Repression offered the possibility of quick results but at the risk of exacerbating Italian anglophobia. The more liberal alternative might fail to achieve its purpose in time. Despite the pressure of much military opinion, Brigadier Kennedy-Cooke, the head of the new British Administration, approached the problem realistically and dispassionately. In simple terms he sought to win the acquiescence of the Italian civil population in British authority by friendly and generous treatment and by the tactful presentation of the British point of view as a counter to Fascist propaganda.

Most Italians were living under pitiful and seemingly hopeless conditions. With the influx of refugees and fugitive soldiery, the Italian population had increased from 40,000 to 70,000 men, women, and children. Most were living in Asmara, where sanitary conditions were deplorable and the supply of water was inadequate. Many were destitute, either because they were now unemployed or, in the case of several thousands of women and children, because their husbands and fathers had been killed or captured; food was scarce; prices were rising. Each problem was tackled urgently and energetically. Several thousands of refugees were evacuated to the smaller towns, systematic billeting was introduced, and additional accommodation was made available by the repair of buildings damaged during the campaign. The Royal Engineers increased the Asmara water supply; the Royal Army Medical Corps introduced town cleansing services and enforced sanitary regulations; and the Royal Army Service Corps imported essential supplies for the civil population. At the same time the unemployed and destitute were registered, and paid relief from British funds. These measures were, of course, palliatives and could not secure the Italians against all distress and discomfort: they did, however, spare them famine and disease.

It was against this background of humane and, in the circumstances, comparatively generous treatment that Brigadier Kennedy-Cooke sought to combat Fascist influence by lending the British the appearance of caretakers rather than of conquerors. 'Fraternization', as it was termed, was officially encouraged. Boxing and football

The British Impact on Eritrea, 1941–50

matches were organized between British and Italian teams; British officers and Italians met in the congenial surroundings of an officially sponsored tennis club. The Italians, though volatile, were incapable of long-sustained hatred and the British, if phlegmatic and perhaps at times a little arrogant, were not insusceptible to the attractions of civilian society. In time Italian sullenness and British frigidity began to thaw out.

But fraternization alone would never have weakened Fascist influence sufficiently. There was a need also to combat Fascist ideas and win some understanding of the British point of view. To this end a daily newspaper the *Quotidiano Eritreo* or *Eritrea Daily News* was published. With the proscription of the former Fascist press it was assured a wide circulation, but its effectiveness derived from the moderation with which its British editors presented their arguments and the pains they took to respect Italian susceptibilities. They resisted the temptation of countering the vulgarities of Fascist propaganda with crude attacks against Fascism and its leaders, and sought instead to divorce Italian national pride from Italian faith in Fascism. While loyalty to the Duce and patriotism were still synonymous terms, open attacks on Fascism would have offended national honour and kindled faith in Fascism. There was nothing in the *Quotidiano Eritreo* to offend the Italian patriot unduly. By presenting facts accurately and without undue elaboration it left the Fascists to discredit themselves by the very extravagance of their claims and assertions.

By such means most Italians were quietly induced to acquiesce in British authority and view Fascist propaganda, if not with complete disbelief at least with increasing indifference. There remained, however, an incorrigible hard core of Fascist hot-heads who still constituted a threat to security. Their identification was not easy but, thanks to the efforts of a small and zealous Intelligence Section, most became known to the Administration within a few months. The more dangerous were quickly interned, but action against the majority was deferred until the Italian temper was judged to have improved sufficiently, seven months after the beginning of the occupation. The eventual arrest and internment of 3,000 undesirables in November 1941 threw out small ripples of interest but otherwise left Italian society unmoved.

By the close of 1941 the danger that Eritrea might prove an expensive military commitment had passed. Though the curious hybrid administration functioned somewhat awkwardly, the essential business of government was adequately discharged. The apparent ease with which British authority had been established belied the narrow-

Eritrea

ness of the margin between what was comparatively inexpensive success and what might have been costly failure. It was fortunate that an officer with such intuition as Brigadier Kennedy-Cooke had charge of the Administration. It was fortunate also that, during this difficult period of transition, he was able to call on the services of a small but invaluable body of officers seconded from the Sudan Government. Their flexibility, gift for swift assessment, and invariable sang-froid did as much as anything to secure British authority at so small a cost.

THE SYSTEM OF GOVERNMENT

There were significant differences between Italian and British authority in Eritrea. Italian authority had rested on the sovereignty of the Italian Crown; British authority derived from international rules governing the occupation of enemy territory in war time. Italian authority had been designed for a colony which it was believed would remain Italian indefinitely; British authority was of a provisional nature, its life depending, first, on the outcome of the war and, secondly, on the terms of an eventual peace treaty. Also, Italian authority had been engaged in a policy which was at complete variance with British ideas of colonial government.

Because of these differences the system of government which the British found on their arrival was not in all respects suited to their purpose. Certain features were inconvenient; others undesirable. But, whatever the British might have desired, their hands were tied by the terms of the Hague Convention of 1907, which denied to an authority occupying enemy territory in war time the right to change existing institutions and laws, except for reasons of military necessity, humanity, and conscience. And so the British had little freedom to introduce formal changes to suit either their convenience or mood until the war had ended. But then, as we shall see, their hands were no less firmly tied by the problems of the Peace.

Though the head of the British Administration, eventually known as the Chief Administrator,[2] assumed the position of the former Italian Governor, his authority and status were less. The Italian Governor had been the representative of the Italian Crown. The Chief Administrator was not the representative of the British Crown nor, until the last few years of the Occupation, had he any right of correspondence with a British Secretary of State. His status varied according to the circumstances of war and peace. While Eritrea was

---

[2] Known as Deputy Chief Political Officer until August 1941 and as Military Administrator until March 1943. Thereafter the title of Chief Administrator was employed.

The British Impact on Eritrea, 1941–50

still technically an area of military operations, he was no more than an officer on the staff of the General Officer Commanding in Eritrea, who was directly responsible to the Commander-in-Chief, Middle East, for the civil government of the territory. Subsequently, he took over the civil government in the name of a Chief Civil Affairs Officer[3] on the staff of the Commander-in-Chief. It was not until 1949, when responsibility for the occupied Italian colonies was transferred to the Foreign Office and the appointment of Chief Civil Affairs Officer was abolished, that the Chief Administrator had direct contact with a department of the British Government.

The transfer of responsibility to the Foreign Office also brought about a welcome change in the character of the Administration. Until then it had been a military Administration and both the Chief Administrator and his officers had held commissions in the Army. This arrangement had made for a singularly awkward relationship between the Chief Administrator and the commander of the military garrison.[4] Both held the same rank of Brigadier; fortuitously the military commander was invariably the senior of the two; and, to make matters worse, he had disciplinary authority over all officers in the territory including the Chief Administrator and his staff. No arrangement could have been calculated to cause more unnecessary and damaging mischief. Once responsibility for Eritrea passed to the Foreign Office, the Administration lost its military character, its officers discarded their military commissions, and, by tacit consent, the military commander conceded precedence to the Chief Administrator.

The transfer of responsibility to the Foreign Office also improved the position of the Chief Administrator by bringing under his direct authority two groups of departments which had been largely outside his control since the beginning of the Occupation. Previously the head of the group of departments responsible for financial and economic matters, the Deputy Controller of Finance and Accounts, and a Legal Adviser who was responsible for legal and judicial matters had been directly responsible, first, to GHQ, Middle East, and then to the War Office. Now they became directly responsible to the Chief Administrator.

The quasi-independent status of these officers had until then relieved the Chief Administrator's principal executive officer, the Chief Secretary, of responsibility for some of the more important subjects which had fallen within the orbit of his Italian counterpart, the

[3] Known as Chief Political Officer until March 1943 and thereafter as Chief Civil Affairs Officer.
[4] In August 1941 the General Officer Commanding was succeeded by an Area Commander. During 1949 the title was changed to that of District Commander.

25

Eritrea

Secretary General. The departments of Finance and Accounts, Trade and Supplies, Customs and Excise, and Revenue and State Lands were all in the charge of the Deputy Controller of Finance and Accounts: the Legal Department, which included the judiciary and the equivalent of an Attorney General's department, was controlled by the Legal Adviser, who was also responsible for the department of the Custodian of Enemy Property. In other respects the British Chief Secretary's appointment was analogous to that of the Italian Secretary General. The heads of the remaining departments of the Administration and the executive officers in charge of the administrative divisions into which the territory subdivided were each under his direct control. The Secretariat and departmental organization resembled the Italian; and, in some instances, the British took over the former Italian departments intact.

As we have seen, the Italian police forces—the quasi-military and royalist *carabinieri* and the Fascist *Polizia Africana Italiana* were disbanded during 1941. The Eritrean police force which took their place was manned by officers who were British, an inspectorate which, though British at first, later included Eritreans, and a rank and file which was Eritrean. Though the force was not designed to admit an Italian cadre, the presence of a large Italian population made it difficult to do without one. In the event a small section of Italian police was recruited from the *carabinieri* and attached to it.

The territorial structure of the Italian Administration remained substantially unchanged; and was only modified where a lack of administrative staff left the British without practicable alternatives. The Italians had divided the territory into seven administrative 'divisions' or *commissariati* (Hamasain, Akelli Guzai, Serai, Keren, Agordat, Massawa, and Assab), which were each subdivided into varying numbers of districts or *residenze*, which, in some instances, were subdivided yet again into sub-districts or *vice-residenze*.[5] This arrangement was designed to serve the Italian need for direct and close administration, and demanded more than twice the number of officers required for an equivalent responsibility in a British colonial territory. And so when, for reasons referred to later in this chapter,[6] Italian officials were removed from administrative appointments, the Italian organization had to be tailored to the British staff available by the elimination of all *vice-residenze* and two *commissariati*.[7]

[5] In the charge of officials known as *Commissari*, *Residenti*, and *Vice-residenti*.
[6] See below, p. 30.
[7] The Massawa and Assab *commissariati* were amalgamated as the Red Sea Division in 1943, and the Keren and Agordat *commissariati* were converted into the Western Province in 1947.

The British Impact on Eritrea, 1941–50

The Italians had instituted no system of local government in the usual sense of the term. They had, however, established what were formally described as municipalities in the seven principal towns.[8] In each, the local administration was in the charge of a *Podestà* or mayor appointed by and responsible to the Governor. There was no council of any kind and the only feature distinguishing the municipalities from government departments was the right to collect revenue and administer independent budgets. As a matter of administrative convenience the British allowed the municipal administrations in the two largest towns, Asmara and Massawa, to continue functioning; the others were eventually taken over by the Administration, on the ground that they had become insolvent.

During the Italian régime the judiciary administered four types of law: the Italian Penal Code, which was applicable to all the inhabitants of the territory; the Italian Civil Code, which extended to all civil issues where at least one of the parties was an Italian citizen; the *Sharia* or Islamic Law, which obtained in certain civil issues where the parties were Moslems; and Eritrean customary law, which, in its appropriate form, was enforced in each civil case between Eritreans.

Jurisdiction in penal cases had reposed in five courts: the *Giudice della Colonia* or Judge of the Colony in all cases involving Europeans, the courts of the *Commissari* and *Residenti* in all but the more serious categories of penal cases involving Eritreans and other non-Europeans, and the *Tribunale del Commissariato* or Tribunal of the Commissariat in most of the more serious categories of penal cases involving non-Europeans. The most serious of this last category were referred to a *Corte di Assise* or Assize Court. Europeans had a right of appeal to an Appeal Court for Italian East Africa in Addis Ababa. Appeals lodged by non-Europeans lay to the Governor.

Jurisdiction in civil issues was shared by several authorities. The Governor alone could determine what were known as 'collective disputes' between Eritrean village, clan, or tribal groups. Civil issues between individual Eritreans of the same religion and community lay within the jurisdiction of the appropriate village or clan heads, as judges in the first instance, 'district' or tribal chiefs, as judges in the second, and *Commissari* or *Residenti* as judges in the third. Civil issues between individual Eritreans, who were not of the same religion or members of the same community, were determined directly by the *Commissari* or *Residenti*. Certain types of civil issue between Moslem Eritreans came within the jurisdiction of the *Sharia* or Islamic courts. All civil issues involving Europeans lay with the

[8] Asmara, Massawa, Keren, Decamere, Addi Ugri, Addi Qaieh, and Assab.

27

Eritrea

Judge of the Colony. Appeals from the Judge of the Colony lay to the Appeal Court of Italian East Africa. Appeals in all cases involving Eritreans, other than those from the *Sharia* Courts, which lay to a *Sharia* Court of Appeal, were to the Governor.

This highly complex judicial system was not fully suited to the circumstances of the Occupation. Though the Italian courts could be expected to exercise jurisdiction in many cases arising out of British Proclamation Law, in war-time it was unreasonable to call upon them to adjudicate in matters relating to the maintenance of British authority. To obviate this difficulty a Standing Military Court[9] was established, with jurisdiction in all penal cases involving either British or Italian law. It was composed of British officers, who were empowered to sit individually or collectively as panels of the court in different parts of the territory simultaneously; a single officer constituting a panel of the court except in the more serious cases, where it was composed of three officers. Subsequently Native Courts, on which panels of Eritrean chiefs and notables sat, were also established, with the same jurisdiction in civil issues as the *Commissari* and *Residenti*, and with a limited jurisdiction in penal cases. The Standing Military Court and the Native Courts functioned side by side with the former Italian authorities: the Judge of the Colony, the Tribunal of the Commissariat, and the Assize Court; and, with the progressive removal of Italian officers from administrative appointments, a dwindling number of *Commissario's* and *Residente's* Courts. The British and Native Courts disposed of most cases involving Eritreans; and, with few exceptions, the jurisdiction of the Italian courts was limited to cases where the parties were Europeans.

The dissolution of the Appeal Court for Italian East Africa in 1941 necessitated a further modification of the Italian system. In its place there was set up an Italian Court of Civil and Criminal Appeal with jurisdiction in the case of all appeals from Europeans against the decisions of subordinate courts. Appeals from non-Europeans lay direct to the Chief Administrator, who in this and other respects inherited the powers of the former Italian Governor.

The British system of government was in many respects anomalous and untidy. The long dependence of the Chief Administrator on a Chief Civil Affairs Officer, the awkward relationship between him and the military commander, the quasi-independent status of the Deputy Controller of Finance and Accounts and Legal Adviser, the coincidence of judicial and executive responsibilities, the multiplicity of judicial authorities and their overlapping jurisdiction, and the

[9] The title was changed to British Court in 1949.

The British Impact on Eritrea, 1941-50

cosmopolitan staff of British, Italians, and Eritreans serving the Administration created a variety of problems and difficulties. The system was not designed to conform with any blueprint but evolved by improvisations and expedients through a process of continual makeshift adaptation to circumstances. No blueprint could have envisaged what the circumstances of the Occupation would be, whether they would vary, and, if so, when and how they would change. The desirable had inevitably to be subordinated to the practicable in circumstances which precluded any forecast of what would be practicable from one moment to the next. Incongruous though many of its features were, the British system served its purpose.

To the inhabitants of Eritrea, the change in régime brought little apparent change in the system of government. The various processes of government continued much as they always had, and the governmental structure looked little different to all but the more perceptive. The restrictions of the Hague Convention, the difficulty of recruiting adequate British staff, and a variety of political considerations provided obstacles to any radical reform. The reforms the British introduced were none the less radical. They did not affect the system or machinery of government but the purpose for which it was operated.

SOCIAL AND POLITICAL DEVELOPMENT

Before the First World War Italian policy had not differed substantially from that of other colonial powers, but, whereas their outlook subsequently became more liberal, Italy's, under Fascist influence, became more reactionary. In Eritrea the Italian citizen was a principal; the Eritrean an auxiliary. The Eritrean was required to produce inexpensive raw materials for Italian industry, to work for Italian enterprises as a cheap labourer, and to serve in Italy's colonial army as a low-paid mercenary. He remained subject to discriminatory legislation; he had no voice in his country's government; he was not associated with the Italian Administration except in subordinate posts; and what he derived from the social and public services was markedly less than his reasonable entitlement. And yet there was no Eritrean discontent. It was averted by a calculated policy of 'bread and circuses'. Food and consumer goods were always cheap and plentiful; taxation was at a token rate; and largesse was poured out in a rich shower of presents, doles, gratuities, honours, and sinecures. Throughout the Italian régime the Eritrean remained content, docile, and obedient to his rulers.

The British had good reason to modify practices and a policy which so clearly contradicted the principles for which they stood.

Eritrea

The main obstacle to reform was the Italian administrative staff dealing with Eritrean affairs. It would have been unreasonable to have expected *Commissari* and *Residenti* accustomed to Italian methods to participate in a crusade against them. Once British authority had become firmly established, discreet efforts were made to concentrate responsibility for Eritrean administration in British hands. During 1941 the recruitment of British officers was so slow that little progress was made. In the following year German victories in the Western Desert left the officers of the British Administration of Cyrenaica temporarily available for use in Eritrea. Though Italian *Residenti* continued to exercise judicial powers in the Plateau divisions until 1946 and in Asmara until 1949, direct responsibility for Eritrean administration was assumed exclusively by British officers during 1943 and 1944.

The first major problem was posed by the Racial Law and a body of subsidiary legislation designed to enforce racial segregation, confer social and economic privileges on Italian citizens, and generally uphold the principle of 'white superiority'. There was every justification for the immediate annulment of this whole body of offensive law. But at a time when the temper of the Italian population was a matter of anxious concern to the Administration, there was much to be said for leaving matters as they were. In the event, the Administration adopted a prudent and cautious course. At first no formal action was taken but British administrative and police officers were tacitly instructed that none of the discriminatory laws should be enforced. Subsequently as each became a dead letter it was formally repealed.

The gradual removal of the colour bar was accompanied by various measures to associate the Eritrean with the government of his country. Colonial governments are instinctively cautious in conceding responsibility to a native population and, in Eritrea, there were good grounds for hesitancy: the inexperience and lack of education of most Eritreans, their ignorance of English, which was the working language of the Administration, and the fact that, with their past Italian associations, they could not quickly win British confidence. As against this, the British could not afford to be over-cautious. British officers were difficult to find; Italian officials were expensive and politically unreliable. There were obvious attractions in a policy of limited 'Eritreanization'.

During the first few years of the occupation a large number of official appointments previously held by Italians were filled by Eritreans. For the most part they were comparatively subordinate posts —those of public-health assistants, medical orderlies, telephonists,

The British Impact on Eritrea, 1941–50

linesmen, senior clerks, accountants, agricultural supervisors, and so on—but their Eritreanization was a necessary first step. Later on Eritreans were appointed to positions of greater responsibility. First, they were introduced into the inspectorate of the police force and, secondly, some were made Administrative Assistants, appointments which corresponded with those of *Residenti* and *Vice-Residenti*. The political significance of these measures was far greater than was apparent from the comparatively small number of Eritreans who actually obtained advancement. It made public British recognition of the Eritrean's right and ability to acquire control of his own affairs.

Further steps were taken in the same direction. The first was the setting up of Native Courts to replace the *Residenti's* courts. It was an innovation which was widely welcomed, both because it extended Eritrean control into an important aspect of Eritrean affairs and because these Courts disposed of judicial business more quickly and no less satisfactorily than the notoriously dilatory courts of the *Residenti*. Unfortunately, Native Courts were not immediately instituted throughout the territory, since the Legal Adviser ruled that they could only be justified in terms of the Hague Convention where the Residential Courts had ceased to function: a point of view which found no understanding amongst Eritreans and little sympathy amongst officers of the Administration.

The Native Courts constituted a direct challenge to the Italian system of local administration. Italian policy had demanded no more than an executive instrument which would effectively translate government orders into action and, for this purpose, had preferred obedient government agents to chiefs or councils likely to reflect an unpredictable and perhaps inconvenient public opinion. The Italian-appointed chiefs had been required to assess and collect taxes, to act as subordinate judges in certain categories of civil cases, and to execute government orders. So long as they performed these duties satisfactorily they were, within limits, assured of government support, which both rendered them independent of popular feeling and encouraged them in arbitrary and irresponsible behaviour. Though they were mostly corrupt, avaricious, oppressive, and unpopular, their word had been law and their loyalty to the Government absolute.

They were singularly ill-suited to further the purposes of British policy. Abuse of power, irresponsible behaviour, and corrupt practices were detected and then terminated or, at least, modified. At the same time, chiefs were required to assume greater official responsibilities. They were made members of Native Courts, appointed to the chairmanship of educational committees, placed in charge of rural-development schemes, and appointed to Advisory Councils. They were persuaded and coaxed to take an interest in the welfare of their people, to look into their grievances and find out what they needed. Above all they were urged to act on their own initiative and not solely on the orders of the Administration. Results were often disappointing. Old dogs could not be expected to learn new tricks quickly or competently. A few chiefs cultivated some sense of responsibility; some proved incorrigible and were eventually dismissed; the majority did their awkward best to humour their new masters.

Even so the British had a revolutionary effect on the Eritrean. The Italian district officer had usually been remote from the Eritrean. Few had made a practice of touring their districts or acquired more than a superficial knowledge of Eritrean customs and ways; during the fifty years of Italian rule less than a dozen had learned any Eritrean dialect. All this was changed after the Occupation. British officers toured their districts methodically and continuously; they made themselves accessible to all comers; several carried out sociological inquiries and, in a surprisingly short time, collected and recorded much detailed information about tribal and village society, local custom and usage. They got to know the Eritrean villager and tribesman more intimately than their Italian predecessors. And, by getting to know them, they encouraged the Eritreans to think and speak for themselves, with the consequence that the chiefs found themselves having to answer to an emergent public opinion as well as to the Administration.

At the same time Eritrean Advisory Councils were set up in each division and in the principal towns. At first they were composed almost exclusively of chiefs; they had no constitutions; they observed no rules of procedure; and their debates amounted to little more than exchanges of opinion between their members and the British Divisional Officers presiding over them. Subsequently, prominent persons known to enjoy popular support were appointed. As a result, the councils began to develop as the vehicles of Eritrean opinion they were intended to be. They assumed their most elaborate form in the Western Province, where a provincial council and subordinate rural and urban district councils were set up in 1949. The membership, rules of procedure, and powers of these councils were regulated by constitutions which invested them equally with the power to advise the Administration and a right to be consulted by it on a wide range of subjects. In addition some 'rural district councils' administered 'tribal funds' and had powers to legislate within the sphere of local customary law.

The behaviour of the councils was often disappointing. They

seldom displayed any interest in the humdrum details of public administration. All too often their members played to an uninformed gallery by submitting specious proposals without any regard to their financial or administrative implications, by voicing grievances without suggesting practicable remedies, and by refusing to be associated with any measure which, however necessary, was likely to be unpopular. But even so, among many frivolous and impracticable proposals, some useful advice was given; chiefs began to heed public opinion; and where in the past 'the Government' had been an alien institution, personified in Eritrean eyes by some European official, it now became something which, through the councils, could be more easily approached and influenced.

Political advancement underlined the Eritreans' need for education. Before the Occupation there had only been twenty-four primary schools.[10] The standard of teaching had been low; its scope designedly narrow.

By the end of his fourth year [wrote an Italian Director of Education], the Eritrean student should be able to speak our language moderately well; he should know the four arithmetical operations within normal limits; he should be a convinced propagandist of the principles of hygiene; and of history he should know only the names of those who have made Italy great.[11]

The only schools which aspired to more normal standards were those provided by the Swedish Evangelical Mission. They were closed by order of the Italian Government in 1932.

Italian neglect left the British with a formidable task. There were no trained teachers, no suitable school text-books, and only a few school buildings. Also the funds which the Administration could make available were severely limited. Each problem was tackled and in time a modest educational edifice was erected. At first a few schools were opened with the help of a small number of trained teachers recruited from the Sudan and from the few Eritreans with higher education; later, other schools were opened as pupil teachers became available, and finally, after a system of teacher training had been introduced in 1943, a steady flow of trained teachers was fed out to the schools. Arabic text-books were obtained from Egypt and the Sudan, and, later, others in Tigrinya were prepared and printed by the Administration. Where there were no school buildings, funds were raised by voluntary subscription and the schools were built. By

---

[10] Four Power Commission of Investigation for the Former Italian Colonies, Vol. I, *Report on Eritrea* [in later references, *Four Power Commission Report*] (1948, mimeo), p. 69.

[11] Confidential direction to Italian headmasters by Signor Festa, Director of Education in Eritrea, in 1938.

Eritrea

1950 the Administration had set up a middle school and fifty-nine primary schools.[12]

During the Italian régime instruction in the schools had been in Italian; and because of this and of Eritrean contact with the Italian population, a surprisingly large number of Eritreans had a fair knowledge of colloquial Italian. There was much to be said for continuing to use Italian, but because the Administration needed English-speaking Eritreans and because the younger Eritreans themselves demanded to learn English, Italian was abandoned. In their last year at primary schools children were taught English and at the intermediate and, eventually, secondary levels English was used throughout. The choice of a language of instruction at primary schools was left for decision by local educational committees, which invariably favoured the use of Tigrinya, where the local population was predominantly Christian, or Arabic where it was Moslem.

Educational development aroused an unexpected enthusiasm amongst a large number of Eritreans. Not only were parents ready to make substantial sacrifices to send their children to school but, in the towns, the young and even the middle-aged clamoured to be given the opportunities denied them during the Italian régime. To meet this adult demand English Institutes were established, first at Asmara and then in the other towns. English was taught by British officers and English-speaking Eritreans and Italians; lessons were given in typing and shorthand; discussions, lectures, concerts, gramophone recitals, and film shows were arranged; and, with the help of the British Council, a useful library and a supply of English periodicals were made available. Despite a somewhat greater concern with Italian affairs, the Ministry of Information also provided various educational and cultural facilities for Eritreans and published weekly newspapers in Tigrinya and Arabic.

The Administration also ensured that the Eritrean should enjoy greater benefits from the local health service. Previously an elaborate medical service, nine superbly equipped hospitals, and sixty-three dispensaries had mainly served European interests. Hospitals and dispensaries had been sited in the principal European centres; few if any facilities had existed in towns and districts without substantial European communities. As against 800 Eritrean beds there had been 1,200 European beds.[13] In the towns where 'municipal cleansing services' had functioned, they had only operated in the European quarters: the native quarters had been cleansed by the communal efforts of their Eritrean inhabitants or, more often, left in a condition of increasingly insanitary neglect.

[12] *Four Power Commission Report*, p. 71.   [13] Ibid. p. 72.

The British Impact on Eritrea, 1941-50

The British Administration provided the Eritrean with better facilities. By 1950, as against 440 European beds in the hospitals, there were 1,400 Eritrean beds. Thirty-two new dispensaries were functioning in rural districts and a number of mobile dressers were serving among the nomadic tribes. In the towns a newly constituted public-health service was responsible for all town cleansing. In the malarial districts of the lowlands malaria-control squads were employed to combat mosquito breeding. And finally nine clinics for the care and treatment of Eritrean children were opened under the auspices of an Eritrean Children's Welfare Society, a quasi-official organization established in 1943 on the personal initiative of the Chief Administrator, Brigadier S. H. Longrigg.[14]

In themselves the British reforms were modest and unspectacular. An official colour bar was removed, Native Courts and Advisory Councils were set up, a few Eritreans were appointed to responsible but minor positions in the Administration, a humble educational service was in being, and the health service was functioning to the greater advantage of the Eritreans. And yet what had been done was revolutionary. For the first time as a colonial people the Eritreans were associated with the government of their country; after half a century of political sterility they were being encouraged to think for themselves and assume responsibility. Also they were being taught, and were beginning to learn, the hardest lesson in any subject people's political primer: that responsibility carries with it financial obligations. The old days of 'bread and circuses' were over. The Eritreans were now contributing to the cost of schools and dispensaries by voluntary subscriptions and the payment of school and medical fees; they were being made to subscribe to the cost of administration by substantially increased taxes and, for the first time, by the payment of municipal rates in the towns.

This revolution was undertaken by the small band of British officers in the Administration. They had been recruited haphazardly, and included individuals with every kind of background and experience. Because of the unpredictable course of the war and the demands of other occupied enemy territories, their arrivals and departures were seldom planned and their residence in Eritrea was usually brief. It might not be supposed that as temporary caretakers they would have cultivated any real interest in their task. And yet it was their enthusiasm that enabled the Eritrean to advance so far and so swiftly. Their efforts were co-ordinated and directed by Brigadier S. H. Longrigg, who, as Chief Administrator from 1942 until 1944, both moulded the Administration into its new form and

[14] Ibid. pp. 72-74.

Eritrea

so integrated and manipulated its diverse and apparently inconsistent mechanisms as to enable them to operate harmoniously and purposefully. More than any other British administrator in Eritrea he could claim to have been both the author of British policy and the architect of the Administration itself.

Economic Development

The occupation of enemy territory imposes an irksome responsibility for its administration and welfare on the Occupying Power. If the territory is rich there is the compensation of economic benefits: if it should be poor the Occupying Power's own resources may be weakened to the prejudice of its military strength. In Eritrea the British found themselves in occupation of a territory which boasted very modest resources and was in a state of economic collapse.

It had never been Italian policy to develop Eritrea's few assets. Italy had looked on Eritrea as a clearing-house from which Italian manufactured goods were distributed to Ethiopia, the Sudan, and Arabia in exchange for the raw materials needed by Italian industry. In this scheme there was no place for any Eritrean development or enterprise which might compete with Italian industry or prejudice Italy's export trade.

With the Italian conquest of Ethiopia in 1935, Eritrea was converted into a base for the exploitation of the Ethiopian hinterland. During the following five years military installations, public buildings, workshops, depots, warehouses, offices, shops, blocks of flats, villas, and encampments were rapidly thrown up. The port of Massawa was enlarged, and linked with Asmara by one of the longest cable-ways in the world. A magnificent network of roads was constructed to supplement the little mountain railway and the few rough tracks which had formerly linked Asmara with the territory's main centres. Modern airports were built at Asmara and Gura; and a number of satellite landing-grounds were laid out elsewhere. All this was carried out by an army of Italian officials, engineers, mechanics, artisans, professional men, and traders, who arrived in the territory after 1935; it was made possible by large-scale imports of mechanical and constructional material and a lavish investment of Italian capital.

As a result Eritrea was placed in a state of almost complete economic dependence on Italy. With the European population increasing from 5,000 to 50,000 in five years and a rapidly expanding Eritrean urban population with a higher standard of living than before, there was a growing demand for consumer goods; and yet, because nearly all development was constructional, the Eritrean was no

The British Impact on Eritrea, 1941–50

better placed to meet it. Consequently the gap had to be bridged with subsidized Italian imports. With the Occupation the subsidized Italian enterprises closed down and Italian imports ceased. The awkward problem confronting the British was how to find work for thousands of Italian and Eritrean unemployed and supply a territory which was far from self-sufficient and had little to export.

Fortunately for Eritrea the war had created a scarcity of trade goods in the Middle East, where a demand was growing for a wide range of goods which had formerly been imported from Europe. In Eritrea there were plant, equipment, and stocks of raw materials; there were the territory's neglected local resources and a labour force of high quality. Given sufficient respite to readjust its economy, Eritrea could find salvation in the Middle Eastern market.

This was provided fortuitously by the victories of Field-Marshal Rommel in the spring and summer of 1941. Because of the threat of air attack, British GHQ Middle East was anxious to move some base installations from Egypt. Eritrea had more to offer than territories such as Palestine, the Sudan, and Kenya. It was out of range of German aircraft and yet was only three days' safe sailing from Egypt; it had a modern port at Massawa and excellent internal communications; Europeans could be comfortably accommodated on the Plateau in a congenial climate; and it disposed of labour, plant, and equipment. Plans for utilizing these assets were considered in the summer of 1941 and in the winter work began.

Most of the military projects took the form of American aid, provided, at first, by an American firm, Johnson Drake & Piper, Inc., working under the control of American military and civil-aviation authorities and, later, after America's entry into the war, by the United States army. The Americans constructed an aircraft-assembly plant at the airport of Gura; converted workshops in Asmara into a repair base and an Italian military store at Ghinda into a major ammunition depot for the Royal Navy; established a naval base at Massawa (in co-operation with the British Administration), and modernized the commercial harbour. The British at the same time established a centre at Asmara for the repair and maintenance of BOAC aircraft and erected two base hospitals.

These projects provided work for the unemployed and, by creating a domestic market with high purchasing power, provided the stimulus for the development of a light industrial economy. During 1941 the few industrial enterprises operating before the Occupation had been restarted: throughout 1942 and 1943 Italian ingenuity and enterprise exploited the situation to the full. Soap was manufactured out of old stocks of copra; beer was brewed from Eritrean and im-

37

Eritrea

ported Ethiopian barley; light wines were distilled from Yemeni raisins; caustic soda was processed from the ash of a plant found in the Coastal Plain; matches were manufactured from local euphorbia and imported red phosphorus; scrap metals were converted into hand tools; local linseed oil was used to manufacture paint; leather goods were manufactured from local hides and skins; and among other commodities which were manufactured in smaller quantities were oxygen, paper, glue, and margarine. Most of these products, were fed into the domestic market but, towards the end of 1943, a fair quantity became available for export.

This was as well, for, with the Allied victories in North Africa during the last months of 1942 and the beginning of 1943, the war projects closed down and their labour force of about 14,000 Italians and Eritreans was paid off. The majority of the Italians and some of the Eritreans were quickly absorbed by local industry. Production increased sharply; and among the new industries which came into being were factories for the manufacture of buttons, pottery, glassware, boots and shoes, and fish meal. In December 1943 an Industrial Exhibition was held at Asmara to advertise Eritrea's potential as a source of industrial supply in the Middle Eastern market. The value of exports subsequently rose from £494,000 in 1943 to £1,678,000 in 1945.[15]

This industrial boom was the product of exceptional conditions and could not be expected to survive the favourable climate of war. Few Eritrean industries could withstand European competition after 1945. Machinery was wearing out and replacements were often unobtainable; the pre-war stocks of raw materials were running out; labour and transport costs were increasing; and additional handicaps were emerging in the form of currency restrictions. In general, European goods were cheaper, of better quality, and delivered more promptly and in more certain quantities. One by one most of the new Eritrean industries which had sprung up since 1942 closed down or reduced production to meet domestic needs. To an increasing extent Eritrea was thrown back on its own resources: its livestock, agriculture, forests, marine wealth, and minerals.

Eritrea's principal source of natural wealth has always been its livestock. Though rainfall is scarce there was sufficient grazing in the past to support large herds and flocks of camels, goats, and sheep, so long as they migrated seasonally between the regions of summer and winter rains. Their quality was, however, affected by animal diseases—mainly rinderpest and trypanosomiasis—and uncontrolled breeding.

[15] *Four Power Commission Report*, Appendix 64B.

The British Impact on Eritrea, 1941-50

The Italians had developed an efficient veterinary service, and had established a Vaccine Institute (a research institute and vaccine factory), which combated disease with such success that livestock doubled in quantity between 1905 and 1940.[16] Even so, little was done to exploit the country's potential wealth in animal by-products; and, throughout the Italian régime, milk, butter, and cheese for the European population were imported from Italy.

After the Occupation the British set about exploiting local resources as best they could to compensate for the loss of Italian imports. As a start a Milk Section was established by the Administration's Agricultural Department, and under its supervision sufficient milk was collected and pasteurized from local Eritrean herds to satisfy the local European demand. In time the European demand for butter and cheese was also met and, for a while, a small surplus of cheeses became available for export. Pig breeding was encouraged with stock imported from Kenya, and by 1945 there were as many as 25,000 pigs in the territory.[17] The heavy demands of the urban population were met without difficulty; indeed, with the continuing increase in livestock, the threat of overstocking became serious.

With the exception of a few relatively small areas, Eritrea does not lend itself to any large-scale agricultural development. Rainfall is generally scarce, capricious, and torrential; and less than 3 per cent. of the territory's land surface is cultivated. The best agricultural land lies in the Gash-Setit Lowlands where, however, domestic water is scarce, the climate uncongenial, and malaria prevalent. Though the Plateau and the southern districts of the Northern Highlands offer more favourable conditions, the mountainous nature of the terrain and increasing soil erosion have restricted cultivation to small, fertile patches. The deserts of the Baraka Lowlands and the Coastal Plain are only cultivable along the flanks of the main watercourses.

Physical diversity has permitted the cultivation of a variety of crops. In the highland areas the principal crops are wheat, barley, and an Abyssinian millet known as *taff*; in the lowlands *dhurra* (sorghum), *dukhn*, and maize. Production, however, is on a comparatively small scale, and yield rates are low, both because of the indifferent quality of the soil and because of the incompetence of the Eritrean cultivator. Many Eritreans have only recently taken to

[16]

	Cattle	Goats and Sheep	Camels
1905	296,000	736,000	47,000
1940	591,000	1,491,000	68,000
1946	1,200,000	2,200,000	105,000

SOURCE: *Four Power Commission Report*, p. 40.

[17] Ibid., pp. 40-41.

Eritrea

agriculture and even cultivators of long standing often use methods which are primitive and destructive.

Italian policy was mainly concerned with producing cash crops for the Italian market. Nine experimental stations were established and research was carried out at two laboratories in Asmara, mainly for the benefit of Italian agriculturists, who were also helped with loans and marketing facilities by a state Agrarian Bank and an Agricultural Association. The most successful enterprise was a parastatal organization which produced an average crop of about 280 tons of cotton on about 5,000 acres near the Sudan border. Tropical fruits, sisal, and coffee were also grown for export to Italy, but on a small scale. Nothing, however, was done to encourage the production of grain or vegetables, in which Eritrea was deficient and dependent on imports.

Because the war had made it difficult to import foodstuffs the British endeavoured to make the territory self-sufficient in vegetables, fruit, and grain. Ten thousand acres were given out in concession to Italian market-gardeners and by 1950 they were not only meeting the local European demand for fruit and vegetables, but were exporting a small surplus to Aden and the Dhahran oilfields in Saudi Arabia. The cotton plantations on the Sudan border were converted to the production of grain, and extensive riverain lands in the Coastal Plain were irrigated and developed as grain-producing areas. At the same time efforts were made to increase the productivity of the Eritrean cultivator by propaganda, the establishment of demonstration plots, and, in some areas, the provision of tractors and motor ploughs. The most effective stimuli to production, however, were the return of thousands of ex-soldiers to the land and the incentive of the high prices that agricultural produce fetched in the local market. By 1946 640,000 acres were under cultivation as against 141,000 acres in 1939; the grain crop being 118,000 tons as against 28,500 tons.[18]

The only trees of commercial value were the dom palms in the Baraka Lowlands, which provided raw material for the manufacture of buttons; the *Euphorbia candelabra* in the Plateau and the Northern Highlands, from which matches were made; the *Boswellia papyrifera*, in the Northern Highlands and Gash-Setit, which provided a crude but commercially valuable incense; and various acacias, principally in the Gash-Setit Lowlands, from which gum arabic was extracted. The Italian Government's main concern was to conserve what little forest land was left, and this it did through an efficient corps of forestry guards. The British continued to employ the same corps and

[18] *Four Power Commission Report*, App. 33.

The British Impact on Eritrea, 1941-50

to pursue much the same policy as the Italians, though they tended to place a greater emphasis on afforestation, in an effort to repair losses of timber and counteract soil erosion.

The Red Sea has been a traditional source of Eritrean wealth in salt, pearls, mother-of-pearl, and fish. During the Italian régime salt-pans were established at Massawa and Assab by a private company with monopoly rights; similar rights in fishing and pearl fishing were also granted to other private companies. Production was at a high level, and a large proportion of Eritrea's exports was made up of marine products. After the Occupation the salt works continued to function as before but the fishing industry slackened off. The fishing fleets had suffered war damage and, because of the high prices and rates sea craft fetched during the war years, many vessels were either sold or engaged in transport work. The industry had also suffered as a consequence of the British requisitioning of mechanical equipment which later proved difficult to replace. The industry was almost at a standstill before 1944, but later on more ships became available and, by 1950, fish meal and mother-of-pearl were accounting for one-eighth of Eritrea's export trade.

Eritrea's mineral resources have not been exhaustively surveyed but from available evidence they seem to be of small value. Modest quantities of gold have been found on the Plateau and in the Gash-Setit Lowlands; the gold content of veins standing at 9 grammes to the ton in the Gash-Setit Lowlands as against 4-5 grammes on the Plateau. Deposits of iron ore estimated at 17 million tons lie in the foothills behind Massawa; nickel, copper, white asbestos, manganese, titanium, magnesium, chromium, mica, vermiculite, kaolin, and feldspar are also to be found in different parts of the territory, but they are either insufficient in quantity or too remotely situated to justify exploitation. Large quantities of sodium and potassium salts exist in the southern stretch of the Coastal Plain, but the best deposits lie well inland within the Ethiopian border.

The Italians put much effort and capital into gold mining and during the 1930's drew up an ambitious plan for the exploitation of the Gash-Setit, which they initiated with some lavishly equipped mine works at Ugaro. By 1940 gold production had risen to an annual rate of 17,000 oz. and the industry showed promise of development. Then most of the mechanical equipment in the mines was requisitioned, dismantled, and removed by the British and American military authorities soon after the beginning of the Occupation. Replacements were difficult and often impossible to obtain. Though a few mines reopened during and after 1945, production was low, the annual output only averaging about 3,000 oz. Later, after 1948,

Eritrea

insecurity and political terrorism brought the industry to a standstill. Also, because of Eritrean claims to rights in land, the Administration found it necessary to restrict prospecting to a point where it was all but prohibited.

Unfortunate though the deterioration of the mining and fisheries industries was, its economic implications were not unduly serious. The Administration's main concern was to find adequate supplies of foodstuffs and consumer goods and to provide the new industries with sufficient raw materials. Agricultural development reduced the gap between supply and demand; and light industrial development reduced Eritrean dependence on imported consumer and manufactured goods. Even so, in 1947, it was estimated that Eritrea needed to import 34,600 tons of foodstuffs, 32,000 tons of fuel oils, and 5,200,000 square yards of textiles to meet its requirements.[19]

The task of provisioning Eritrea was a source of continual British anxiety during the war years. Italy was cut off until 1947; trading with a recently liberated Ethiopia was barely possible before 1944; the produce of the Yemen was largely reserved for Aden; and even as late as 1950 the Sudan was forbidding the export of cereals. At first the Administration imported supplies through the Army supplies and transport organization, but, towards the end of 1942, responsibility passed to the United Kingdom Commercial Corporation and remained with it until 1944. The problem, however, was largely solved by private enterprise, which found sufficient incentive in the high rate of purchasing power to import enough trade goods from Aden and grain from Ethiopia to meet Eritrea's needs.

To ease the supply problem the Administration was concerned to find a means of ridding Eritrea of the large unproductive element in the European population made up of women, children, and infirm or unemployed men. During 1941 about 20,000 men were interned as prisoners of war and shipped to South Africa, India, and Kenya. During 1942 and 1943 about 10,000 men, women, and children were repatriated to Italy by arrangement with the Italian Government. After the end of the war about 10,000 more Italians left the territory, either at their own expense or at that of the Italian Government. By 1950 the European population had decreased from its 1941 figure of 60,000 to 20,000.

Agricultural and industrial development had little effect on Eritrea's habitually adverse balance of trade. During the Italian régime exports had only averaged about 50 per cent. of imports. Before 1947, when imports were limited and Eritrean industrial products could find markets abroad, exports averaged about 57 per cent. of

[19] *Four Power Commission Report*, App. 67.

The British Impact on Eritrea, 1941–50

the value of imports; thereafter they dropped to about 50 per cent. By 1950 the balance of trade had in fact reverted to very much what it had been before the Occupation. Equilibrium was realized, as it had been in the past, through the transit trade. Eritrea continued as an entrepôt centre for the re-export of primary products from Ethiopia to world markets, either raw or after processing, and of oil fuels, textiles, and other trade goods to Ethiopia. Between 1947 and 1949 the annual value of this trade averaged about £3,000,000, or almost as much as the annual value of all imports, and nearly twice as much as that of exports during the same period. As in the past, Eritrea's most valuable economic asset continued to be its geographical position.

FINANCE

The military and provisional nature of the British régime, its emphasis on Eritrean social and political development, and the changing economy of the territory were variously reflected in British financial administration. The nature and extent of public revenue and expenditure were each affected and, with them, the welfare of the territory.

When the British entered Eritrea the currency resources of the four Italian banks[20] had been reduced to 15 per cent. of their deposit values, largely as a consequence of the Italian Government ordering them to destroy their stocks on the eve of Asmara's occupation. Consequently, the British took immediate steps to restrict their activities. They were all required to hold reserves covering, at first, 100 per cent. and, after 1943, 50 per cent. of all deposits, and were not allowed to issue loans of more than £1,000 in any one case. They were also prevented from dealing in foreign exchange. Because of these restrictions, Barclays Bank (Dominions, Colonial & Overseas), which was the only British concern functioning in the territory, came to assume a special status in the local schemes, since it acted as bankers for the Administration and became a central bank for all dealings in foreign exchange and the holding of British currencies.

During the Italian régime the Eritrean budget had only been balanced by grants-in-aid from the Italian Government, which amounted to four-fifths of revenue between 1910 and 1920, and one-half between 1920 and 1930; and, in the absence of records, must be presumed to have exceeded local revenue between 1930 and 1940. And so the British found themselves committed to maintaining a standard of administration and public services out of all proportion

[20] Banca d'Italia, Banco di Roma, Banco di Napoli, Banca Cooperativa Popolare Eritrea.

to the territory's resources at a time when they proposed to improve the lot of the Eritrean and, consequently, to spend more money on him. Since they had no reason to subsidize an occupied territory, for which they were only caretakers, at the high rate set by the Italians, they had to solve the problem by resorting to every reasonable means of increasing revenue and reducing expenditure.

The Italians had kept direct taxation low and, as a matter of policy, had placed the main burden on the European population. The principal direct taxes were income, property, and municipal taxes and what was known as 'native tribute'. Though many Eritreans in the towns were liable to income, property, and municipal taxes, few if any were ever called upon to pay them. Native tribute was payable collectively by tribes and groups of villages through their chiefs. Though a form of income-tax, there was no recognized basis for its assessment and, in practice, assessments varied as be-between one community and another. Its incidence, however, was remarkably light and did not average more than the equivalent of threepence per head of population. More than half the territory's revenue from direct taxation was collected as income, property, and municipal taxes; native tribute accounted for barely an eighth.

Revenue from indirect taxes was mostly derived from customs and excise or from profits on state monopolies for tobacco and the manufacture of matches. Italian policy had been to protect imports of Italian origin and to encourage trade between Eritrea and Ethiopia by exempting goods moving between them from customs duty. Since most imports were of Italian origin and Eritrea's trade was mainly with Ethiopia, only about a tenth of general revenue was realized from indirect taxation.

To increase revenue the British had to abandon some of the basic principles of Italian policy. First, they required Eritreans to contribute their fair share to revenue. For the first time Eritreans had to pay income, property, and municipal taxes and also school and hospital fees. At the same time, native tribute was reassessed on a more realistic basis, the average payment per head of population being raised to about one shilling and threepence.

The only other major step the British took to increase revenue was to levy what were known as 'contributions': an expedient permitted by international law on grounds of necessity. 'Contributions' were levied annually on all incomes liable to tax after 1942 and on all registered motor vehicles after 1946. They were also levied on certain types of imports.

Though committed to greater expenditure on social services than the Italians, the British did what they could to economize. Expendi-

The British Impact on Eritrea, 1941–50

ture on capital works was all but completely eliminated and the maintenance of assets such as roads, railways, ports, and public buildings was limited to what was essential. Pensions owing from the Italian Government were not paid; many sinecures which were no more than disguised pensions for services to the Italian Government were abolished; and redundant staff were progressively dismissed until, by 1948, the Administration was employing less than half the number of Italians and Eritreans who had served the Italian Government in 1940.

The British had reason to congratulate themselves on what they achieved. Though the budget was only balanced once, in 1950, and then fortuitously, the United Kingdom Government was only called upon to pay subsidies amounting to a total of £1½ million between 1941 and 1950. Adequate banking and exchange facilities were furnished; and the essential services of government were provided and in some respects improved. It was, however, to be expected that a policy of strict care and maintenance should cause some injury.

The lira savings of many Italians and Eritreans were reduced to about a sixth of their pre-occupation value as a result of the conversion from Italian to East African currency:[21] loans could only be obtained with difficulty and at high rates of interest; taxes had been increased and their incidence was more widespread; many Italians and Eritreans who had been public pensioners or employees of the Italian Government had lost what had been assured incomes; the Italian and Eritrean employees of the Administration were poorly paid; large-scale development projects which might have brought long-term advantages to the territory could not be contemplated; and certain capital assets, such as the railway and some roads and public buildings, deteriorated owing to inadequate maintenance. In a financial as well as an economic sense the Occupation brought with it a cold wind of depression; it was this which so largely, though variously, influenced the emergent political thought of Italian and Eritrean alike.

[21] Conversion was at the rate of 480 lire to the £ as against the 1940 Italian rate of 83·65 lire.

III

THE GROWTH OF POLITICAL CONSCIOUSNESS, 1941-7

URBAN XENOPHOBIA

No less than 180,000 Eritreans, or about one-fifth of the Eritrean population, live in towns, and at least three-quarters of this number reside in Asmara and its satellite Decamere, the towns which developed most rapidly under the impact of Italian activity during the late 1930's. The other towns became somewhat larger during this period, but otherwise retained their earlier character. Massawa and Assab remained seaports; Keren, Addi Ugri, Addi Qaieh, Agordat, Barentu, and Tessenai remained administrative centres and rural market towns. Asmara changed from a comparatively small administrative centre into a large modern town, which was housing some 50,000 Europeans and 120,000 Eritreans by 1941.

The social structure of Asmara had significant peculiarities. Society broke down into European, Asian, and Eritrean racial groups, but each had characteristics which lent it a somewhat more complex weave than is usual in multiracial colonial communities. The Europeans, or Italians as they mostly were, comprised an amalgam of social classes and were not the conventional European settlers, officials, and business men fringed thinly about by a few technicians—but a whole community in themselves. The Arabs were traders and shopkeepers; but, within the petty bourgeoisie to which they belonged, there were also Abyssinian Moslems or Jiberti. The majority of the Eritreans were labourers, white-collared workers, and artisans. Most, also, were Christian Abyssinians.[1] Here then was a society shaped by race, religion, and occupation and composed in the main of Italians, Moslem Jiberti and Arabs, and Christian Abyssinians: a society where race and religion indicated the occupation and class of the individual and determined the stresses and strains to which each was susceptible.

The Christian Abyssinians comprised more than two-thirds of the Eritrean population; socially and economically, however, they were the weakest element in it. During the Italian régime they had not been dissatisfied. The novelty of town life, good wages, and cheap

[1] Mainly Tigrinyans from the Plateau, including a fair proportion of immigrant Ethiopian Abyssinians.

The Growth of Political Consciousness, 1941–7

consumer goods had dulled their wits. A deliberate, and indeed cynical, policy of keeping the Eritrean's belly full and his head empty had earned the Italians political tranquillity. During the Occupation the process was reversed. Eritrean heads were now filled with new ideas gleaned from lectures and books provided by the English Institute and British Information Office, the weekly Tigrinyan newspaper, contact with Indians and Sudanese serving in the British forces, and the liberalism of British administration. Influences of this kind, married to the economic distress which followed, bred discontent and then political consciousness.

No group was hit so severely as the Christian Abyssinians. The military and civil enterprises provided most Italians with employment and high wages; the boom which followed industrial development favoured the Jiberti and Arab merchants; the Christian Abyssinians found nothing but unemployment, or employment at starvation rates of pay. The demand of the military and civil enterprises for skilled as against unskilled labour was proportionately higher than that of the pre-war constructional projects; the pressure for quick results gave employers an understandable preference for the ready-made Italian technician or artisan as compared with the untutored and often unreliable Eritrean. In the event employers had to pay high wages to get skilled Italian labour, while Eritrean labour, being plentiful and unwanted, was cheap. To add to the Eritrean's discomfiture the cost of living had increased to almost six times the 1940 figure by 1944, as against a 60 per cent. rise in wages over the same period. Such was the grim background against which the Christian Abyssinians of Asmara struggled to exist.

White-collared workers tend to suffer most at such times. And so it was the Eritrean clerks, office boys, mechanics, and others who had emerged from the ranks of manual labourers to acquire sophistication of a kind, and, even more, those who had served in the Italian Administration, who felt the change in climate most keenly. Though the Italian Government had only offered Eritreans subordinate positions with limited opportunities of promotion, they had enjoyed a living wage, a leisurely existence, positions of honour and usually of privilege, retirement on pension, and, in the case of the more favoured, appointment to chieftainships and sinecures. Each had a vested interest in the service commensurate with the credit which he had accumulated with his Italian masters.

With Italian defeat all this was lost. A record of loyalty to the Italians was calculated to excite British suspicion rather than approval; and proficiency in the use of Italian counted for little in an Administration which now worked in English. Overnight the currency of past service depreciated as long years of endeavour lost their former value. At the same time despite the opportunities offered to the more capable Eritreans in the British Administration, service within it was generally much less attractive than it had been with the Italian Government. The pay bore little relation to the cost of living; one employee was expected to do what two had formerly done; most of the privileges conceded by the Italians were denied by the British; no pensions were paid; and clerical service ceased to be the conventional means of advancement to chieftainships and sinecures. The condition of most who remained to serve the British Administration was miserable; it was enviable by comparison with that of the thousand or so whom the British found it necessary to dismiss for reasons of economy.

For the unemployed the struggle for existence was bitter and humiliating. The majority had retained property and rights in their villages, amounting in each case to a few head of cattle, some goats, and a share in the village lands. Few, however, were now fit to start life anew as peasants; and most continued, as in the past, to lease their land in return for a share of the crop. The livestock they sold piecemeal to fill the recurring gap between what they needed and what they obtained from their tenants. Many who had been in government service as clerks or soldiers had accumulated what, by Eritrean standards, were substantial cash savings in lire. Many, too, had arrears of pay owing to them for their last months of service under the Italian régime. With a little capital there were opportunities for the industrious who wished to enter business in the Eritrea of 1942 and 1943; and, with their cash savings behind them, some might well have found a livelihood in the modest one-man enterprises which were then being exploited almost exclusively by Italians. But, as it was, their capital quickly evaporated. The value of their lira savings had either deteriorated to one-sixth of what it had been in 1940 or had vanished with Italian authority. Their arrears of pay remained unpaid. Most lived, as might be expected, by selling or mortgaging what property they had and by sinking progressively into greater indebtedness.

The intellectual processes set in motion by British methods and propaganda were consequently coloured by growing economic distress. Christian Abyssinian labourers and white-collared workers became increasingly aware of their common plight and thereby of a livelier sense of solidarity than they had ever derived from their common religion. Both felt underprivileged, and both began to demand a greater share in the benefits which their country had to offer. During the Italian régime the Christian Abyssinian worker

The Growth of Political Consciousness, 1941–7

had neither wanted nor found popular leaders, being content to listen to the orders of Government transmitted through the chiefs. Now, the stimuli of hunger and despair made him impatient for leaders who would give words to his feelings and give him hope of a better future, at the same time as a politically conscious intelligentsia with an itch for power began to emerge. The intelligentsia aspired to leadership; the Christian Abyssinian proletariat readily conceded it.

It was something of a paradox that, though it was the memory of the fat years of the Italian régime which so largely accounted for their discontent, the immediate target of the intelligentsia's bitterness was the Italian population. The Italians, now discredited by defeat, could not expect to retain the loyalty and respect which they had formerly enjoyed; they had no reason, however, to anticipate the hostility which first began to froth up around them in 1942. Though the British had not intended to stir up racial hatreds, indirectly their propaganda and methods had brought the Italian régime into contempt. Each new school, each Advisory Council or Native Court, each Eritrean appointed to a post formerly reserved for a European, and each article of colour-bar legislation which was rescinded amounted to an indictment of the Italian régime. The intelligentsia could scarcely overlook the contrast between British and Italian policy or fail to perceive the cynicism of past Italian benevolence. And so the thought of what they had been denied, and what they had consequently become, rankled and filled them with bitterness against their former rulers.

This bitterness increased as their interests came into conflict with their Italian neighbours. When they looked for work, more often than not they now found themselves competing with Italian applicants. All that they could offer to offset the Italians' superior qualifications was their willingness to accept lower wages. When they sought licences from the Administration to run transport services, start charcoal and firewood businesses, sell milk, or manufacture cheese, preference was usually given to Italians who had more capital and greater technical experience than themselves. It was too much to expect them to view the success of their Italian rivals dispassionately. In time they regarded them and all Italians with an unreasoning hatred.

Eritrean hatred came to be directed with peculiar intensity against Italian officials such as *carabinieri* in the police force, judges, and *Residenti*. Because of their unfamiliarity with the Italian penal code, British police officers tended to employ Italian n.c.o.'s on the investigation of crime. Their methods were notoriously rigorous and complaints of extorted confessions and physical maltreatment were neither infrequent nor always unjustified. Similarly, the *Residenti*, who continued to exercise jurisdiction in penal cases involving Eritreans in Asmara until 1947, followed Italian procedure, which showed less favour to the accused than that employed in British courts. The most common grievance, however, arose from the arrangement whereby all civil suits as between Italians and Eritreans were disposed of by Italian judges. The Eritrean was unfamiliar with Italian procedure, he knew nothing of the Italian Civil Code, unlike his Italian adversary he could seldom purchase legal advice, and, often, the fees he was required to pay before bringing a case to court were beyond his means.

There was resentment also against the various technical departments of the Administration, which mostly continued to be served by Italian officials. Minor Italian officials were frequently accused of favouring their own compatriots, and of obstructive officiousness in their dealings with Eritreans. Also, at a time when Eritreans in other branches of the Administration were being given opportunities of promotion, it was exasperating for those in the Italian-controlled departments to find themselves limited to the same ceiling as before.

A subsidiary but serious cause of Eritrean ill feeling was the uxoriousness of the Italian male. The Fascist Government had included certain articles in the Racial Law to protect the purity of the Italian and Eritrean races by prohibiting sexual intimacy between them. These were, however, seldom enforced, and the Eritrean concubine, who was invariably a Christian Abyssinian, became an established element in many Italian households. In many cases the relationship between patron and concubine was coloured by a genuine affection; in others it was no more than contractual prostitution. But, whatever its nature, it came into being because the Abyssinian woman found the Italian male economically more attractive than the Eritrean. This, and the fact that a large proportion of the women were removed from an Abyssinian community where the men were already greatly in the majority, aroused bitterness in the Abyssinian which was particularly directed against the half-castes born of these unions.

Italophobia mainly developed among the intelligentsia, who, as a class, had the closest contact with the Italians; hatred of the Moslem Arabs and Jiberti was almost as intense, but was shown by Abyssinian intelligentsia and proletariat alike. Hatred stemmed from envy and fear. The Moslem trader throve during the first years of the Occupation, when prices were high and opportunities of substantial profits were good. That Arabs should be permitted to pro-

The Growth of Political Consciousness, 1941–7

fiteer at Eritrean expense seemed an unwarrantable injustice. Nor was it any more tolerable that the despised Jiberti should grow fat on profits gleaned from their Christian superiors. But, worse still, the impoverished Christian Abyssinians could only obtain loans or credit by favour of the Arabs and Jiberti. Progressively they became more indebted to their Moslem creditors, losing property to them as mortgages were foreclosed. It was for this reason that the Moslem traders were feared. Being feared and envied they were hated.

The Christian Abyssinian cultivated an equivalent dislike of the Sudanese, mainly garrison troops and labourers who came to work in some of the military enterprises. As Moslems and aliens the Sudanese were regarded with suspicion and, as members of what the Abyssinians believed to be an inferior and, as they would say, blacker race than their own, with contempt. The Sudanese, for their part, were inclined to arrogance, regarding the Christian Abyssinians as a conquered race from whom they were entitled to respect as conquerors. Wherever Sudanese and Abyssinians came in contact there were incidents, ranging from minor brawls to serious riots.

Xenophobia is seldom a selective quality. Hatred for Italians, Arabs, Jiberti, and Sudanese was accompanied by a growing suspicion of British intentions. Under the nagging ache of poverty and unredressed grievances the sophisticated Eritreans began to suspect the British of favouring their enemies. In Asmara, where an Italian municipality was responsible for the local administration, the Eritreans had very much less contact with the British than elsewhere and such as they had was mostly with junior members of the police force and technical departments. In an Administration of such recent origin there was no tradition to cast its stamp on its servants and, though the Administration was, for the most part, surprisingly well served, there was some poor material at the lower levels.

The sophisticated Eritrean was highly sensitive, suspicious, and plagued with complexes. To probe beneath the crust of his self-assertiveness and insolence required a perceptiveness and intellectual background which few junior British officials had. Also few had had the experience to enable them to strike the right note of sympathy and firmness in dealing with the intelligentsia. There is no doubt that many sophisticated Eritreans in Asmara had reason to complain of discourteous or inconsiderate treatment, and consequently to believe that the Administration had a prejudice against them. They were puzzled and angered by the contrast between British treatment of Eritreans in Asmara and elsewhere.

In Asmara, the Italian system remained for the most part unchanged: elsewhere, it had largely been superseded. The Italian

Eritrea

municipality carried on as before and, though an Advisory Council was set up in 1942, it had no formal voice in municipal matters. No Native Courts were set up in Asmara, where *Residenti* continued to administer justice until 1947. Whereas Italian members of the police force were largely withdrawn from other parts of the territory, a comparatively large number were stationed in Asmara. No Eritrean class was better fed with British liberal ideas than the Asmara intelligentsia, none was so starved of British reform.

Rural Discontent

The Occupation had as revolutionary an effect on the Abyssinian peasantry on the Plateau as on their urban kinsmen. The liberalism of British methods encouraged villagers long accustomed to Italian paternalism to think for themselves; with the added spur of economic distress they acquired a lively, if immature, political consciousness. Though their environments differed and their problems were not directly related, peasant and townsman became united in a fortuitous alliance by their common grievances and aspirations. Both had suffered from the change of régime; both came to view Italians and Moslems with bitter hostility; both lost faith in British good intentions; and, eventually, both turned to the same leaders for guidance.

Throughout the Italian régime there had been a continual and, after 1935, remarkable flow of population from the Plateau villages to Asmara and the other towns. Because they were nearer and were by nature more gregarious, the Abyssinian peasantry had responded to the call for soldiers, clerks, artisans, and labourers in very much larger numbers than the Moslem tribesmen. Their exodus from the Plateau valleys brought about important changes in the local economy, society, and land tenure. The process of change had been sufficiently smooth and ordered during the Italian régime for society to adjust itself to it but then, in 1941, it was brought to an abrupt, injurious halt.

The drift to the towns had, in fact, reprieved the Abyssinian peasantry from the consequences of a natural poverty and an increasing population. Thanks to the generous flow of cash remittances from the wage-earners in the towns, their families in the villages were able to preserve, if not improve, their standard of living.

An immediate and serious consequence of the Occupation was that the flow of remittances was suddenly reduced and at the very time when there was a rise in prices and in the cost of living.

A further consequence of the Occupation arose out of certain changes which had taken place in village society and land-tenure forms during the Italian régime. Whether resident in a village or absent in the towns a *restenya* or member of a landowning family retained his entitlement to a share in the village lands. If he were absent, he would arrange for his portion to be worked by a tenant; but, because so many of the landowning class were also absent, tenants had often to be found from outside the village and, indeed, from outside the Eritrean Plateau. In consequence, throughout the Italian régime, landless immigrant families—mostly from the Tigrai in Ethiopia—drifted into the Plateau to settle as tenants of absentee landowners. And so village communities which had once been composed almost wholly of landowning families came in time to absorb so many *makalai ailet* or tenants that the latter often outnumbered the *restenya*.

Once admitted to a village community, a *makalai ailet* family was permitted by an out-of-date, but unquestioned, custom to remain there and enjoy perpetual usufructory rights in the land. This meant that, as with successive generations the number of *makalai ailet* increased, the village community had to provide them with plots in a progressively decreasing area of uncultivated land. Within most Plateau villages land had been held communally by the landowning families or *enda* in the villages. As land grew scarce they began to trespass on each other's lands, to quarrel, fight, and sometimes kill to defend or further their interests. To ease friction the Italian Government had in many cases converted the system of land tenure from a family to a village basis, thereby extinguishing family rights and sharing out the land as equitably as possible among the village community as a whole.

This resulted in new problems after the end of the Italian régime. Although many of those who had left their villages went back after 1941, there was no compensatory exodus of *makalai ailet*, who were by this time entrenched in the villages with perpetual usufructory rights. And so, at a time when the peasant was confronted with rising prices and the partial loss of his urban remittances, the pressure on his land increased sharply and suddenly. A population of approximately 388,000 was left with barely 440,000 acres of cultivable land at its disposal.

It was not surprising that the peasant cast hungry eyes on the Italian farms and market gardens sited on what was held to be *demaniale* or Crown land, but was nevertheless invariably land in which Eritreans had or claimed long-established rights. Italian law had empowered the Governor to declare certain specified types of land *demaniale*, provided that he gave adequate notice of what he proposed to do. In practice, the provisions of the law were often ignored, or unwittingly misapplied, by *commissari* who, in their zeal

Eritrea

to further Italian agricultural development often allocated land to Italian agriculturists which had never been formally declared *demaniale*. All too often no hearing was given to local objections, and Italian ignorance of Eritrean land tenure was the frequent cause of violations of traditional rights. In the Eritrean Government's annual report for 1913 the Italian Governor, Ferdinando Martini, wrote

> In my previous report I did not conceal the serious consequences of the hasty appropriations of land by the State and particularly of those lands which were taken without any account being taken of local customary rights. Native opinion cannot understand how the Government is able to appropriate lands which have always been private property.

In all some 70,000 acres were acquired by Italian agriculturists before the Occupation. By comparison with the scale of land alienation in other parts of Africa this may seem trivial. But in Eritrea it was largely excised from the few cultivable acres of the Plateau, since it was there alone that the climate favoured European settlement. Every acre so alienated was claimed by some Abyssinian community on the grounds of incontestable customary rights. The British had of course no legal power to liquidate rights acquired during the Italian régime and no alternative to maintaining the *status quo*. This came as a shock to the Plateau communities; so did the alienation of a further 10,000 acres to Italians during the first three years of the Occupation.

The British, though anxious to protect Eritrean rights, were subject to unusual pressures. The local European population—Italians, British, and Americans—needed fruit and vegetables and many unemployed Italians needed a livelihood. Because of this the British did their best to allocate as much land as possible for vegetable and fruit production to those best qualified and equipped to use it.

To the peasant, land alienation under the British seemed as unjust as it was during the Italian régime. At the beginning of the Occupation British officers knew very little about Eritrean land tenure, the records of the Italian land office were often uninformative and such advice as was available was usually unreliable. It was easy to assume that uncultivated or unoccupied land was state property.

Thus, for example, many fertile stretches of uncultivated land flanking the small streams which traverse some Plateau valleys were leased to Italian smallholders, and turned to profitable account by pump-irrigation schemes. Little did the British officers concerned suspect that Eritreans had irrefutable claims to most of the land; and that it was left uncultivated, by reason of ancient custom, to give livestock easy access to water.

The Growth of Political Consciousness, 1941-7

It was in ways such as this that Eritrean rights were often violated to the advantage of the Italian agriculturist. Consequently suspicion, fear, and hatred of Italians spread. Friction between the Italian farmer and his Eritrean neighbour increased as the one became exasperated at continual straying cattle, pilfering, and trespass, while the other grew bitter at the sight of alien hands working his soil. Of the many incidents which took place between 1941 and 1944, two were of particular significance. In 1942 the valuable fruit gardens which a certain Kantibai Tesfamariam had leased to an Italian were wantonly ransacked and destroyed. In 1944 an armed gang butchered two Italian farmers in cold blood and then ransacked their property. These were not acts of brigandage but of a sinister patriotism which sought to drive the Italians from Eritrean land and to punish their Eritrean friends.

Italophobia was also aroused in other ways. Whenever Italians tried to cut firewood, burn charcoal, quarry for stone, or prospect for minerals they met with bitter and often blind opposition. The natural resources of the territory were too limited and too valuable to be exploited except by those with the knowledge and means to work them effectively. Few Eritreans had the knowledge or means to do so and, as a consequence, most concessions of this kind were obtained by Italians. The Administration, it is true, forbade mineral prospecting except with the consent of the owners of the land, but all it achieved by doing so was to restrict an activity which might otherwise have brought the territory much-needed additional wealth.

In any event the Abyssinian peasantry had to expand or starve; and, in this plight, the spacious and thinly populated lands of the Moslem tribes beckoned invitingly. Any mass migration to these lowland prairies was precluded by the Abyssinians' distaste for the intense summer heat and their fear of malaria. Expansion took two forms. Herds and flocks were dispatched in increasing numbers to the lowlands during the summer, when the land on the Plateau was under cultivation. Secondly, much of the land fringing the Plateau was either occupied or claimed by neighbouring Abyssinian villages. As a consequence the Abyssinians came rapidly into conflict with the two largest Moslem tribes, the Saho Assa'orta in the east and the Tigray Bani Amir in the west.

This occurred at the same time as the Abyssinian peasant found himself seriously embarrassed by the mounting debts he owed the Jiberti traders. There had been extraordinary peasant indebtedness before the Occupation; but, by 1944, whole villages had mortgaged their crops before they had been sown. To an intolerant and backward population the Moslem Jiberti was even more of an outcast

Eritrea

than in the towns. Relations between the Christians and their Moslem creditors deteriorated, accentuating their differences to a degree unknown during the Italian régime.

Surprisingly, the British Administration did not earn much unpopularity for its alienation of land: it was mainly criticized for its handling of collective land disputes between tribes and villages. In Italian times such disputes had been determined by the Governor on the advice of the *Commissari* who, before reporting, usually set up committees of chiefs and notables to inquire into the disputes and advise them. Since the Governor invariably required additional information involving reference back to the *Commissari* and, through them, to the committees of inquiry, the process was protracted and in some cases years passed before any decision was made. Because of this the British Administration found itself saddled with a disagreeable legacy of outstanding disputes.

During the Occupation the position was further aggravated. The change of régime resulted in the revival of many old claims, and the growing pressure on land to a spate of new disputes. To accelerate the disposal of the many outstanding cases, the Governor's powers were delegated to administrative officers who thereupon became the sole inappellable authorities to dispose of them. The officers exercising these powers were often comparative newcomers, with little knowledge of Eritrean land tenure or custom. On this account they could be excused the errors many undoubtedly made, and, had those who were affected by them had a right of appeal, it is possible that no great harm would have been done. But, as it was, there was no right of appeal. It was incongruous that there was no such right in such cases though they might involve hundreds or even thousands of acres of land; there was, however, a right of appeal against the decisions of Native Courts even though only a few shillings might be at stake.

A further source of grievance was the Administration's fiscal policy. The Italian system of assessing and collecting native tribute had been haphazard and easy-going. The *Commissari* would make a collective assessment for each tribe or Plateau 'district' (group of villages), and the chiefs would then collect what was demanded of them in return for a *pourboire* of 10 per cent. of the amount collected. The assessments were arbitrary; and, in practice, political considerations—which, for example, accounted for extremely light assessments in the case of the Abyssinian communities on the Ethiopian frontier—were often a decisive factor. There was no recognized scale at which chiefs might collect, no receipts were given, and the whole system invited large-scale abuse.

The Growth of Political Consciousness, 1941–7

While assessments had been little more than nominal during the Italian régime, no very great harm had been done. Unfortunately, in their anxiety to increase revenue, the British increased native-tribute rates without reforming the system. The officers in charge of the divisions were required to increase the rates but their recommendations were influenced more by the problem of collection than by the ability of communities to pay.

And so the settled Abyssinian peasantry who were economically least fitted to bear the burden were taxed at the highest rate, while the elusive Tigray nomads who had suffered very little from the economic depression were the most lightly assessed.

Nevertheless though the Administration was not spared criticism, it never earned a fraction of the bitter feelings it had incurred in the towns. The Abyssinian peasant was disappointed and indeed somewhat hurt that an Administration which had in so many other ways shown such consideration for him should parcel out his land to Italians, tolerate profiteering by Jiberti traders, deal so arbitrarily with land disputes, and be so severe in the matter of taxes. Disappointment did not breed anger so much as disillusionment as to British intentions. If his wrongs were to be righted and he was to have any prospect of prosperity, he now knew he would have to find leaders of his own. The prestige and influence of the 'district chiefs' was no longer what it had been. As their power to act arbitrarily diminished under British administration, their authority waned also. Now that he had less reason to fear his chief the peasant found less cause to respect or obey him. In the event he looked to Asmara, where the intelligentsia were beginning to speak the kind of language he could understand and in a tone nicely attuned to his mood.

Ethiopian Nationalism

A colonial government usually directs its efforts to a recognized end, such as dominion status, integration with the metropolitan country, or independence. In Eritrea the British had no notion how or when the country would be disposed of. They knew only that Eritrea's fate would be decided by the Allies when they signed a peace treaty with Italy; and that, until then, British responsibility for this small, impoverished country would continue.

Ethiopia's claims to Eritrea, though by no means irrefutable, were impressive. With the exception of Italy no country could claim comparable historical rights in Eritrea. She could claim to have exercised effective sovereignty on the Plateau before the Italian régime; and if her hold on the Northern Highlands had been brief and tenuous, she could argue that it had been no less effective than the Fungs' and had lasted longer than the Egyptians'. She might have no precise title to the Eritrean Danakil, but as she had conquered and absorbed the rest of Dankali country,[2] it seemed logical that the Eritrean Danakil should be united with their kinsmen in Ethiopia. Similarly the Baria and Kunama were mainly an offshoot of the large Nilotic population of western Ethiopia and belonged there. And as for the Baraka Lowlands, and the northern stretch of the Coastal Plain, they had now become so fully integrated with the rest of the country that direct Ethiopian rights in one part of Eritrea implied indirect rights in the other. The Ethiopian case could also be supported on ethnical grounds. It could for example be claimed that the Plateau folk were Tigrinyans and consequently akin to the other Abyssinians of Ethiopia. They spoke similar languages and like them were mostly Coptic Christians. Though the Tigray clans in the Northern Highlands and adjacent lowlands were Moslems, it could be said that many had once been Coptic Christians and some still observed Abyssinian customs.

There were also economic and strategic arguments in Ethiopia's favour. Economically the two countries were interdependent. Under the stimulus of Italian development, Ethiopia had become as dependent on the port of Massawa, and the storage and transport facilities based on Asmara, as Eritrea had on Ethiopia for grain and raw materials. Strategically, Eritrea was as vital to Ethiopia as the Low Countries had traditionally been to Britain. Within less than eighty years it had served as a base for no less than four foreign invasions: Lord Napier's successful expedition of 1868, the ill-fated Egyptian attempt of 1875, the disastrous Italian invasion of 1896, and the Fascist conquest of Ethiopia in 1935. Alien rule in Eritrea would always constitute a potential threat to Ethiopian independence.

A less valid argument put forward by Ethiopians soon after the Occupation was the allegation that Britain had promised to reunite Eritrea with Ethiopia after the war. This was not based on any formal British declaration but on the texts of various propaganda leaflets which had been scattered from the air during the campaign of 1940–1. The one most frequently quoted was in the form of a proclamation from the Emperor Haile Selassie. The relevant part of the text reads as follows.

Eritrean People . . . ! You were separated from your Mother Ethiopia and were put under the yoke of the enemy, and under the yoke of the enemy you still remain. . . . I have come to restore the independence of my country, including Eritrea, whose people will henceforth dwell under the shade of the Ethiopian flag. . . .

---

[2] The Danakil were included in Ethiopia during the nineteenth century.

The Growth of Political Consciousness, 1941–7

A further leaflet, prepared by the British intelligence, was also quoted

> Eritrean soldiers, listen! Desert from the Italians and join us! We know the reason you would not fight us was that you did not wish to be ruled by the Italians: you will receive your full reward. You people who wish to live under the flag of His Imperial Majesty and to have your own flag, we give you our word you shall be allowed to choose what government you desire!

The British could not be committed by a proclamation from the Emperor; and if the text of the British leaflet was inopportune, and somewhat equivocal, it seems to have implied no more than an imprudent promise that Eritreans would have a say in their future.

Nevertheless the Ethiopians certainly believed that their British allies would do what they could to help them realize their claims. Consequently, the British view that Eritrea was still legally Italian territory came as a profound shock. This, the continued employment of Italian officials in the Administration, and optimistic Italian chatter, suggesting that Italian authority would return to Eritrea no matter what the outcome of the war, aroused the gravest anxiety in Ethiopia. It was not as if she could expect any spontaneous demonstration of pro-Ethiopian feeling in Eritrea. In the past, even the Tigrinyans in Eritrea had, in a political sense, been surprisingly indifferent to their historical links with Ethiopia. Ethiopian irredentism had never caused the Italians a moment's serious concern. No Ethiopian fifth column had emerged in Eritrea after the Italian defeat at Adowa; and when the Italians invaded Ethiopia in 1935, they had received the most loyal and wholehearted Eritrean co-operation.

If they were not to lose their case by default, the Ethiopians had to arouse some Eritrean support. To this end they first turned to the Coptic Church. The Church had always been the custodian of Abyssinian tradition and could consequently be expected to exercise an exceptional influence amongst the Abyssinians of Eritrea and Ethiopia and, in its own interests, to work for their political union. Moreover the Church in Eritrea had a substantial material interest in the matter. Before the Italian régime it had disposed of extensive landed estates, which included the Bahri where fertile soils and near-perennial rains combined to produce the most favoured agricultural land in the country. To the great advantage of a priest-ridden population the Italian Government had dispossessed the Church of these estates, converted them into Crown land, and then leased them to many of the land-hungry Plateau villages and a few Italian settlers. Since then the British had rejected all its petitions for the return of the land. Only union with Ethiopia and the favour of its traditional protector,

Eritrea

the Emperor of Ethiopia, could now restore its property to the Church. Also the Bishop of the Tigrai (and Eritrea), the Abuna Marqos, who had co-operated with the Italians and had been consecrated by an Italian puppet Archbishop,[3] had every reason to be zealous in the Ethiopian cause if he were to retain his see.

By 1942 every priest had become a propagandist in the Ethiopian cause, every village church had become a centre of Ethiopian nationalism, and popular religious feast days such as 'Maskal' (the Feast of the Cross) had become occasions for open displays of Ethiopian patriotism. The cathedral, monasteries, and village churches would be festooned with Ethiopian flags and the sermons and prayers would be delivered in unequivocal political language. The Abuna's Epiphany address in 1942 was characteristic.

> A male child [he then said] is brought into the Church forty days after it has been born and a female child is brought eighty days after birth. Names are then given to them. When the child cries, its mother gives it milk and it stops crying as soon as she lifts it to her breast. But you, my people, have you a name? Yes, you have a mother and you must come to know her as she already knows you.

The clerics spoke in parables but their meaning was clear.

These activities prepared the way for the development of an organized political movement, which was brought about in 1942 by Ethiopian intervention and calculated exploitation of Eritrean grievances. Ethiopia's purpose was served by a procession of young Ethiopian officials who were despatched to Asmara, ostensibly on leave or for the performance of obscure duties. Once in Asmara it was not difficult for them to make contact with the Eritrean intelligentsia. In the coffee houses and taverns their affluence, hospitable disposition, and accounts of the new Ethiopia very soon captivated the disappointed and down at heel and left them bitterly contrasting their own indigence with the visitors' prosperity. The latter were not reticent about Ethiopia's claims to her 'lost province'; nor were they parsimonious in promises of what loyalty to the Ethiopian cause might expect to win.

In the event a society known as the Mahaber Fekri Hager or Love of Country Association, and dedicated to uniting Eritrea with Ethiopia, came into being during 1942. Its membership included most Eritreans who had won the highest favours in the service of the Italian Government, its president, for example, being Gebremaskal Woldu, a comparatively young man who had occupied the most

---

[3] The Abuna Abraham was appointed Metropolitan by the Italians after the Abuna Qerillos had refused to sever relations with the Church in Alexandria.

The Growth of Political Consciousness, 1941–7

favoured position on the staff of the former Italian *Commissario* of Asmara. It lost little time in exploiting the Christian townsman's feelings towards the Italians, Arabs, Jiberti, and British. The tone of its propaganda was attractive: its reasoning convincing. Ethiopia was a country where the Abyssinian was master; where he was not battened on by Europeans; where Arabs, Jiberti, and Moslem tribesmen were under his control; and where the Abyssinian of even modest education could expect to rise to position and power. Propaganda of this kind had a telling effect. During 1942 the aggrieved Asmara intelligentsia was rapidly, if unobtrusively, converted to the Ethiopian cause; by the end of the year the Asmara Advisory Council had acquired a pronouncedly pro-Ethiopian outlook.

Fortuitously this occurred at the time when the victory of El Alamein brought the end of the war into sight. As the Eighth Army thrust westwards during 1943 the Ethiopian Nationalists took more active steps to play on the feelings of the Christian Abyssinians in Asmara. Their campaign was conducted largely by means of posters and pamphlets. Typical of these was one which appeared on the walls of Asmara.

> Eritreans! [it read] Remember your Mother Ethiopia! Your Mother will not deny you and you, her sons, must not deny her. She will feed you. The Italians beat you and dishonoured your women. The British starve you and fatten the foreigners. Have you seen how the Italians and Arabs grow rich while you go naked? Have you seen how the British protect them and despise you? Fools and traitors are saying that the British are your friends and that they wish to help you. Do not believe them. Are the British more likely to help you than the Italians who are of their own race? Are they more likely to help you than their friends, the Sudanese and Arabs? You will find no help except from your Mother. Fight the foreigner and prepare to die for your country. Long live Haile Selassie! Long live Ethiopia!

Propaganda of this kind was well received by the embittered Asmara Abyssinians, who were, at this time, suffering severe hardship from the closure of the American and British military projects. By the time of Mussolini's fall in July 1943 the Nationalist movement had won over most of the Christian Abyssinians of Asmara and the other Plateau towns.

It seems improbable that the Ethiopians were out to pick a quarrel with the British. Some of them suspected that the British favoured a return of Italian authority or, at best, were opposed to Ethiopian claims. Among some British there was undoubted resentment at the challenge to their authority implicit in Ethiopian pretensions and many British officers found it difficult to conceal their dislike of the bitter and touchy young men in the Mahaber Fekri Hager.

Eritrea

The cooler the attitude of the average British officer to the Nationalist movement, the more irresponsibly anti-British it became. The more responsible type of Eritrean, even if privately sympathetic to the Ethiopian cause, was reluctant to join a movement which was becoming increasingly disreputable and the accepted refuge of adventurers, ne'er-do-wells, and the aggrieved. Because of this the movement did not, at first, win many converts in the rural districts of the Plateau. The few who joined it were mostly aspirants to chieftainships, chiefs, and headmen who had been deposed by the Italians and British, notables who had lost sinecures or pensions, and villagers or families who were aggrieved over land disputes. The mass of the population, though emotionally stirred by the activities of their priests, remained politically apathetic.

The chiefs were reluctant to support the Nationalists lest they should displease the British; and yet they did not wish to forfeit Ethiopian favour lest Eritrea should become united with Ethiopia. The majority would have preferred to remain safely on the fence until they knew on which side to alight. Had it not been for the sudden emergence of an opposition movement to the Nationalists during 1943, they might well have done so. Once an opposition had appeared, it was difficult to maintain an enduring neutrality.

The Separatist movement, as it was later known, took root in the Akelli Guzai, the Plateau district remotest from Asmara and the one which had suffered least from land alienation. It was headed by Dejazmatch Tesemma Asberom, the principal chief of the region, and was largely the creation of his son Dejazmatch Abraha, a young chief of outstanding quality and intelligence. Its goal was not at first clear, but it was known to be anti-Ethiopian and pro-British. Though it was ill-organized and had no funds, the movement created a considerable stir among the Asmara Nationalists and Plateau chiefs, who believed it to have been sponsored by the Administration as a counter to Ethiopian nationalism.

However impartial they might try to be, it was natural that British officers should feel better disposed towards those who professed respect for them than towards those who were known to abuse them. Their demeanour did not pass unnoticed; nor did the compliment the Administration paid Dejazmatch Tesemma when it elevated him to the Abyssinian rank of Ras, the highest in the titular hierarchy.[4] That he had deserved the honour by reason of the service

---

[4] Until 1944 the Administration continued the Italian practice of conferring 'titles' on Eritreans as rewards for public service. Christians received Abyssinian titles such as Ras, Dejazmatch, Azmatch, Fitarawzi, and Moslems Turkish titles such as Pasha and Bey.

The Growth of Political Consciousness, 1941–7

he had given was beyond question; that public opinion should interpret it as a British reward for his political activities was only to be expected. In the event Nationalist and, indeed, Ethiopian opinion hardened in a growing hostility towards the Administration. At the same time the majority of chiefs, believing that the British had at last shown their hand, began to intimate their Separatist sympathies.

The Nationalists and Ethiopians were aware that Ras Tesemma and his family were connected by blood and interest with several of the great families of the Tigrai and that they had been closely attached to the notorious Ras Haile Selassie Gugsa, a descendant of the Emperor John who, to win the paramount chieftainship of the Tigrai, had gone over to the Italians. Moreover they believed that some understanding existed between them and Ras Seyum, grandson of the Emperor John and a possible aspirant to the imperial throne. After the death of the Tigrinyan Emperor John, the imperial crown had passed to Menelik, of the rival Shoan branch of Abyssinians, and the imperial seat had been transferred from the ancient Tigrinyan city of Axum to the modern Shoan capital of Addis Ababa. It was natural that the Tigrinyans should be resentful and that their leaders should at times have intrigued to recover the imperial crown. After the Italian defeat in 1941, when rumours were rife that the Tigrai's leaders were planning to secede from the Empire and set up their own kingdom with Ras Seyum at its head, the Emperor took the prudent precaution of holding him in Addis Ababa under careful surveillance. No Shoan Emperor could safely have done otherwise at such a time. It was understandable, therefore, that the Ethiopians and Nationalists should view a Separatist movement with Ras Tesemma Asberom at its head with particular suspicion, believing it to be a British attempt to exploit the known secessionist feeling in the Tigrai.

These suspicions were no sooner formed than a Tigrinyan revolt broke out in August 1943 under the leadership of Blatta Haile Mariam. The insurgents had the advantage of surprise and made a number of impressive gains. A sizeable Ethiopian military force under British command was routed, various administrative centres, including the large town of Adigrat, were captured, and a number of Ethiopian officials took refuge in Eritrea. In the Tigrai and Eritrea it was widely believed that Blatta Haile Mariam had British support, even though the revolt was eventually put down after British aircraft from Aden had bombed the rebels at the Emperor's request.

This took place at the time when Italy was in the process of conversion from an 'enemy' into a 'co-belligerent'. With the war draw-

Eritrea

ing to a close, the emergence of Ras Tesemma's Separatist movement, the apparent British sympathy with this, and the outbreak of Blatta Haile Mariam's revolt assumed in Ethiopian and Nationalist eyes a most sinister significance. It seemed as if the Administration was deliberately planning to ensure its survival: first, by rigging affairs in Eritrea to give the United Kingdom and other Governments the impression that Eritreans preferred British to Ethiopian rule; and, secondly, by exploiting Haile Mariam's revolt to suggest that Ethiopia was unfit to administer Eritrea. A public statement by the Chief Administrator, Brigadier Longrigg, who expressed the 'hope' that when the time came for Eritrea's future to be decided Eritrean wishes would be taken into account, fitted into the supposed pattern of British intrigue; if only because rumours were then current that the Administration intended to invite the chiefs to express their views on Eritrea's future. Had this been so the great majority would unquestionably have declared themselves in favour of continued British administration. As it was, the rumour was false. Even so, the Nationalists took anxious precautions against the eventuality. If the British proposed to get a vote of confidence from the chiefs, they would answer it with a petition from the people. And so towards the end of 1943 the Nationalists, headed by the Abuna Marqos, began to canvass for signatures to a popular petition demanding immediate union with Ethiopia.

Tension mounted in an atmosphere of rumours and suspicion. Up to this point the Administration had been able to adopt an attitude of aloof tolerance towards the Nationalist movement; but now it began to be disturbed by reports of disloyalty amongst some of its Abyssinian employees with known Nationalist sympathies. There was evidence of their co-operation with visiting Ethiopians, of their having stirred up unrest amongst their colleagues, and indeed of having passed on confidential information and documents to Ethiopian agents. But it was the very considerable Abyssinian element in the police force which caused the greatest concern.

The force was barely two years old; it had been hastily recruited; it had no tradition. Promotion had inevitably been determined by individual qualities; and most of those who had gained promotion had been young Abyssinians from Asmara whose higher standard of intelligence had captured British attention. Most shared the Nationalist sympathies of the Asmara intelligentsia; and during 1943 it was notorious that many were in closer contact with the Ethiopians and Nationalists than their duty to the Administration permitted. There were frequent reports of police inspectors and n.c.o.'s attending meetings of Nationalists in the taverns of Asmara. A number had

The Growth of Political Consciousness, 1941-7

also deserted to Ethiopia to be rewarded with senior appointments in the Ethiopian police and army.

A clash between the Nationalists and the Administration was inevitable. It occurred in February 1944 when the Abyssinian members of the Asmara police suddenly staged a 'strike', refusing to go on duty in protest at a change in their footwear from boots to sandals. The reason for the change was that sandals, which were already the standard issue for police elsewhere, were easier to obtain than boots. It was, however, put about and believed that the change implied British contempt for Eritreans. The protest was followed up by an unsigned petition of transparently Nationalist inspiration, in which the strikers demanded the removal of Italian police from the force, the annulment of Italian laws, and the dismissal of Italian judges. The Administration was bound to assert its authority decisively at a time when the war, though ending, had not yet ended. Five prominent Nationalist leaders, including the brother of Ato Dawit Ogbazghi (a senior Ethiopian official and one of the more frequent Ethiopian visitors to Asmara), who were found to have incited the strike were interned and later released after the surrender of sureties. Four police inspectors who were discovered to have been ringleaders were interned. The strikers were then ordered to return to duty on pain of instant dismissal. The strike was broken at once.

The Administration could scarcely have done otherwise. By its action, however, and by subsequently dismissing a large number of active Nationalists in the police force it confirmed the widespread belief that it intended to suppress the Nationalist movement. As a result, the movement received a severe setback. Fear of official displeasure silenced all but the extremists within it and immediately ended the efforts of the Abuna Marqos and his assistants to collect signatures to their petition. At the same time the Separatists, believing that they now enjoyed official favour, became more outspoken. Ras Tesemma convened several meetings of chiefs and notables from different parts of the country, at which the union of Eritrea and the Tigrai as an autonomous state under some form of British administration was openly advocated. The suspicion that the proposal had British approval was sustained by letters in its support which appeared in the British Information Office's weekly Tigrinya newspaper under fictitious signatures; also by the fact that its British-appointed editor, Ato Woldeab Woldemariam, was an outspoken champion of Separatism.

Though the Nationalists were inactive, their cause was now taken up in Ethiopia by the Ethiopia-Hamasain Society, an organization with a supposed membership of Eritrean refugees, which was in

Eritrea

practice known to be financed and directed by the Ethiopian Government. Its declared purpose was the union of Eritrea and Ethiopia, which it ostensibly sought through the collection of subscriptions for a 'fighting fund' and the publication of a weekly newspaper known as *The Voice of Eritrea*. This devoted itself to publicizing the conventional Nationalist arguments, airing the grievances of the Christian Abyssinians against the Italians and Arabs, ridiculing the Separatists, and, above all, accusing the Administration of incompetence, partiality, and oppression. Much of what was printed was, of course, false. Among an immature people it was none the less effective for being so.

Later, *The Voice of Eritrea*, which was published in Tigrinya, was supplemented by an English weekly, the *New Times and Ethiopia News*, edited in the United Kingdom by Miss Sylvia Pankhurst. Its purpose was presumably to win sympathy for the Ethiopian cause among the British public. Nevertheless free copies of it were zealously dispatched to the most unlikely readers in Eritrea, who included illiterate tribal leaders and Italian officials without any knowledge of English. Among the latter a surprised Italian mayor of Asmara received a copy of the paper mysteriously concealed inside a large book entitled *The Peeresses of the Stage*, which had been hollowed out for the purpose by the excision of most of its pages. Whatever impression this presumably costly publication made in the United Kingdom, its value to the Ethiopian cause in Eritrea was negligible.

Nevertheless encouragement from across the Ethiopian border and the free distribution of *The Voice of Eritrea* throughout the towns and villages of the Plateau did much to sustain Nationalist morale after the police 'strike' of 1944. And so the Nationalists, though silent, were on the alert when the great powers began to discuss the Italian peace treaty. The question of the disposal of Eritrea and the other Italian colonies first came up for discussion at the London Conference of the Council of Foreign Ministers in September 1945. As we shall see, the various proposals put forward across the conference table on this occasion showed little sympathy with Ethiopian claims. Nationalist dismay was only rivalled by Separatist jubilation. Towards the end of the year the latter drew up a number of petitions addressed to the Foreign Ministers, in which they demanded British trusteeship for a period of ten years. The signatories were mostly chiefs, with claims to represent the greater part of Eritrea; and though none were from the strongly Nationalist Plateau division of the Hamasain, the Separatist façade was undoubtedly impressive.

If the Nationalists were not to lose their case by default, they would have to bestir themselves to win international sympathy. With

The Growth of Political Consciousness, 1941–7

the evident intention of reviving the movement, the Ethiopian Government appointed a Colonel Negga Haile Selassie as Ethiopian Liaison Officer to Asmara in March 1946. His functions were ostensibly consular in character; and though it was a condition of his acceptance by the Administration that he should not meddle in local politics, he did little to conceal the purpose of his mission. It was soon common knowledge that his headquarters was the meeting-place of the Nationalist oligarchy, that no Nationalist decision could be taken without his approval, and that an increasing number of Nationalist agents were coming on to his payroll.

At the same time the Nationalists launched an exceptionally bitter campaign against the Arabs and Italians. Petitions were submitted in the name of the 'Eritrean People', demanding the immediate expulsion of all Arabs from Eritrea and the dismissal of all Italians from police or administrative appointments. Somewhat irrelevantly, these demands were linked with the 'Eritrean People's fervent desire for union with Ethiopia'. Minor riots caused by Christian Abyssinians broke out in April 1946 in Massawa and Keren, where a few Arabs were injured and some Arab property was destroyed. In June the Ethiopian Government suddenly expelled 130 Arabs into Eritrea after first confiscating their property in Ethiopia. In July a further 145 Arabs and 92 Italians were dumped over the frontier with little more than the clothes on their backs. This action, which was taken without the consent of the Administration, scarcely accorded with the normal rules of international behaviour but, to the Eritrean Abyssinian, it was effective proof of Ethiopia's determination and ability to deal with undesirable aliens.

This campaign of calculated xenophobia was supported by a number of Nationalist demonstrations and processions in the principal towns. Though by law permission was needed for such assemblies, the Nationalists staged them without even seeking authority. At first the Administration did not intervene; but by the time the final procession took place in Asmara on 28 July, it was felt that the Nationalists had gone too far. The procession was broken up and four ringleaders were arrested. Within an hour fierce rioting broke out. The car of the president of the Arab community was set on fire; Arab shops and other property were looted and damaged; and at the same time a mob invaded the police station, where the ringleaders had been incarcerated, and set them free. A further and even more serious riot followed their rearrest and conviction by the Asmara court, and had it not been for the timely intervention of a platoon of the Sudan Defence Force, the small police guard at their prison would undoubtedly have been overwhelmed. As it was, a few rounds were fired, four of the mob were killed, and, immediately, order was restored.

The incident immediately revived the deep-seated prejudices and ill feeling between Sudanese and Abyssinians. On 28 August a few Sudanese troops celebrating the Moslem holiday at the close of the Ramadan fast became involved in argument with some Christian Abyssinians in the Asmara market-place. A Christian Abyssinian mob soon collected and attacked the Sudanese. One was stoned to death; the others escaped to carry the news to their comrades in the barracks. Immediately about seventy of them careered murderously through Asmara's native quarter armed with weapons ransacked from the armoury. During the two hours or so before they were finally brought under control they killed forty-six Christian Abyssinians and wounded more than sixty others. Nine Italians were also wounded.

The similarity between this incident and an occasion when the Fascist Marshal Graziani had once let Italian troops loose in Addis Ababa to avenge the murder of a fellow-countryman, seemed sufficiently close to suggest that the massacre was a British reprisal for the July riots. Bitterness spread rapidly from the towns to the Plateau villages. Though the Church and Nationalists had exploited the peasantry's grievances, it was the wave of indignation following the Asmara incident that swept most of them irrevocably into the Nationalist camp. As in the towns, so now in the villages, most Christian Abyssinians viewed alien European rule with bitter disillusionment and saw no other solution to their problems than Eritrea's union with Ethiopia.

The rural population's conversion was completed at much the same time as the Four Powers at last came to an agreement on the question of the Italian colonies. On 25 September 1946 the Council of Foreign Ministers agreed that Italy should renounce all right and title to her former African possessions and that the Four Powers should decide their future within a year of the Peace Treaty coming into force. Should they fail to agree, the problem was to be referred to the General Assembly of the United Nations.[5] Though the Administration had not prevented the expression of political views up to this time, it had deliberately discouraged the formation of political parties, with the result that neither the Nationalists nor the Separatists were formally organized or indeed free to canvass support publicly. Clearly with Eritrea's future now at stake, and with the prospect of Eritrean opinion being taken into account, there was

---

[5] This agreement was expressed in article 23 and Annex XI of the Italian Peace Treaty (see below, p. 83).

The Growth of Political Consciousness, 1941-7

every need for Eritreans to be given the fullest freedom and, indeed, encouragement to express their views.

During October 1946 Brigadier J. M. Benoy, the Chief Administrator, visited every major centre in the territory and explained to gatherings of chiefs and Advisory Council members what the terms of the Italian Peace Treaty were, leaving them in no doubt that, so long as there was no threat to public order, the Administration would permit the formation of political parties and the free expression of political views.

After this the Nationalist movement was rapidly converted into the Eritrean-Ethiopian Union Party (to be known as the Unionist Party). Offices were set up in every town, and in a short time a fairly efficient party machine had been created under the direction of Ato Tedla Bairu, a young Christian Abyssinian, who until then had served the British as an Administrative Assistant. The party had adequate funds at its disposal, the backing of the Ethiopian Government, and the support of the great majority of the Christian Abyssinian population. It was only opposed by a small disorganized minority in the Akelli Guzai without apparent allies or sympathizers elsewhere. At the close of 1946 the Unionist Party, as it was generally called, appeared to be unchallengeable.

THE MOSLEM MOVEMENT

During the Occupation British opinion had been coming round to the view that the best solution for Eritrea would be its partition between Ethiopia and the Sudan in such a way as to allow the Eritrean Abyssinians to join their kinsmen in Ethiopia and the Moslem tribes of western Eritrea to be incorporated into the Sudan. Sir Douglas Newbold, the Civil Secretary of the Sudan, visited Eritrea during 1943 and came to the conclusion that

> it would be happier for them [the Moslem tribes of Western Eritrea] and no trouble for us [the Sudan Government] to take these two or three districts into Sudan, and let the Christian and Tigrinya speaking districts be reunited to their kinsfolk in Ethiopia.[6]

Brigadier Longrigg held that

> Muslim tribal areas adjoining the Anglo-Egyptian Sudan should be included in that country. The central Christian Highlands with the port of Massawa and the Samhar and the Saho tribes should form part of a United Tigrai state or province, which should be placed under the nominal sovereignty of the Emperor and administered in [the Emperor's] name by a European

---

[6] K. D. D. Henderson, *The Making of the Modern Sudan* (London, Faber, 1953), p. 335.

Eritrea

power for either a stated or an unstated term of years. The Dankali country with Assab should be assigned unconditionally to the Emperor.[7]

Views of this kind were expressed by many others. The partition of Eritrea was also formally proposed by the British representatives at London and Paris in 1945 and 1946.

The weakness of the partitionist argument was that there was no evidence of what Moslem opinion was. Unlike the Christian Abyssinians most Moslems had lived tolerably well after the Italian defeat. On the Plateau the Jiberti traders had prospered, and elsewhere rising prices had been offset by the better opportunities the pastoral tribesmen had found for marketing their livestock and milk. And though there was some unemployment in Massawa after the Royal Navy's base and a cement factory had closed down in 1945, the Moslems in the other towns were little affected by the changing economic climate. Comparative contentment had bred a political apathy which was further favoured by the isolation in which the scattered nomadic tribal groups mostly lived, their obsession with parochial tribal affairs, and their lack of educated leaders.

No significant Moslem movement could develop without the Tigray tribes, who accounted for three-fifths of Eritrea's 520,000 Moslems. Before 1946 they had been too preoccupied with their own affairs to take any interest in territorial politics. The Bani Amir of the Baraka Lowlands had been engaged in a bitter conflict with the neighbouring Hadendowa of the Sudan and in fighting on a less serious scale with the Nilotic tribes of the Gash-Setit. The Samhar clans near Massawa had been concerned to resist claims that the Na'ibs, or traditional chiefs, of Massawa had raised since the Occupation to regain authority over them.[8] In the Northern Highlands aristocratic *shumagulle* families were threatened by an uprising of their serfs. Parochial though these questions were, it was through them and their interplay that the Tigray tribes acquired political consciousness and an Eritrean Moslem movement emerged.

The conflict between the Bani Amir and Hadendowa originated in the latter's claims to the grazing lands lying between the Eritrean frontier and the Baraka. It was natural for these simple folk to infer that, as subjects of the victorious British, the lands they coveted would now be theirs, and for friction between the two tribes to increase. The conflict itself was set off by a Bani Amir named 'Ali

[7] S. H. Longrigg, *A Short History of Eritrea* (Oxford, Clarendon Press, 1945), pp. 174-5.
[8] A family in Massawa had been charged with the administration of the Samhar by the Turks. Its two senior members had been given the title of Na'ib or agent. The Italians limited their authority to Massawa.

The Growth of Political Consciousness, 1941–7

Muhammad Idris, an ex-soldier of the Italian Army nicknamed 'Ali Muntaz or 'Ali the Corporal, who, in reprisal for a petty case of camel theft, headed a large band of raiders and rustled a herd of Hadendowa cattle early in 1942. This was the signal for a tribal war which set the frontier ablaze. Fighting continued off and on for more than three years. 'Ali Muntaz's followers multiplied; their supplies of arms and ammunition remained plentiful; and they raided the Hadendowa repeatedly. The Administration's inability to deal effectively with the outlaws encouraged further disorders in the wild Gash-Setit country, involving the Nilotic Baria and Kunama and immigrant Abyssinian and Bani Amir herdsmen. Peace was restored during 1945 and the early months of 1946. It came first in the Gash-Setit, where the police had always been able to get information from one group against the other. Peace in this region allowed greater attention to be given to the Baraka, where the appeal of outlawry was now diminishing and there was a growing desire for peace. In December 1945 a peace settlement was successfully negotiated. The Bani Amir agreed to pay the Hadendowa several thousand pounds as compensation, and also surrendered about 700 rifles. In return more than 250 of them were pardoned for outlawry. Similar peace settlements were negotiated between the Bani Amir, Baria, and Kunama in the Gash-Setit. None were negotiated with the more elusive Abyssinians, who had by this time mostly taken refuge in the remote Ethiopian district of Addi Abo.

In the meantime trouble of a different kind was brewing in the Northern Highlands. The peculiar feudal structure of the Tigray tribes was an anachronism which began to disintegrate in the climate of Italian defeat and British liberalism. The standard of revolt was first raised by the Tigray serfs of a small tribe called the Ad Taklais, who demanded complete independence and refused to pay the customary taxes or dues. The Administration was sympathetic, but reluctant to indulge in any radical reforms. Nevertheless, to ease the situation, it ruled that the chiefs and *shumagulle* should retain their political authority, but might not enjoy dues and services from the serfs unless these were voluntarily conceded. As a compromise the arrangement was incongruous. To deprive the chiefs and *shumagulle* of their right to dues was to strike at the foundations of aristocratic and chiefly authority.

From 1942 to 1945 the Administration did its best to make an unworkable compromise work. While the Bani Amir and other Baraka clans were preoccupied with the Hadendowa war and their disputes in the Gash-Setit, discontent remained isolated in the Northern Highlands. With the restoration of peace at the end of 1945 it spread from the Northern Highlands to the Baraka. Throughout 1946 British administrative officers reported the serfs' growing demands for emancipation. By the end of the year the Administration found itself faced with a situation where nine-tenths of the Tigray population were united in resistance to the remaining aristocratic tenth.

Unless something was done to satisfy the serfs' demands there was no doubt in the minds of those closest to the problem that administrative control would be lost. There was an urgent need for reform, but it was far from clear what form it should take or how it should be implemented. The heads of the Tigray families were demanding that each little group, sometimes comprising no more than twenty or thirty souls, should become an autonomous political unit. Administratively this was nonsense and if permitted would result in anarchy. If there was to be any administrative order, the serfs would have to be emancipated and organized into reasonably large units.

What form these should take was suggested by a group of ambitious merchants and others of serf origins in the towns of Keren and Agordat, whose spokesman was a former interpreter of the Italian government service named Ibrahim Sultan. They had watched events with interest from the start, but, once British sympathies with the Tigray serfs became known, they came out at the head of a movement for serf emancipation. They suggested that the solution to the problem was to resurrect the ancient Tigray tribes and clans which had disintegrated and disappeared during the sixteenth and seventeenth centuries. To do so seemed an impossible task, but it was the only reasonable means of solving the problem. During 1947 the first steps were taken.

The heads of all Tigray families wishing to be emancipated were invited to meetings where details of their numbers, property, and genealogy were registered. This was not as difficult as had been expected; largely because of the active and not disinterested cooperation of Ibrahim Sultan and his colleagues, who, it was now apparent, aspired to the chieftainships of the emergent Tigray tribes. After the initial inquiries had been completed, meeting after meeting took place to resolve the many differences of opinion and reach agreement on what the future tribal units and their various subdivisions should be. Then chiefs and sub-chiefs had to be elected, disputed elections had to be resolved, and, at the same time, tribute had to be reassessed on a new basis. It was not until the spring of 1949 that the Tigray serfs were completely emancipated. The reorganization had affected a predominantly nomadic population of about 200,000. New chiefs, sub-chiefs, and tribal subdivisions had

The Growth of Political Consciousness, 1941–7

emerged to take their place by the side of the rump of the old *shumagulle*.

To explain how the Tigray–*shumagulle* problem was resolved, we have had to look rather farther ahead than this account of the Moslem movement's development would otherwise justify. What was important was that Ibrahim Sultan and his colleagues had enabled the Administration to advance faster than would otherwise have been possible by co-operating with it, and that their success in winning concessions from the Administration brought the Tigray completely under their influence. In a country where society had always been divided against itself by feuds and conflicting interests, there now emerged a real union embracing all the Tigray serfs. Seeing this, the Baria of the Gash-Setit, who resented paying dues to their chiefs, and the Samhar clans, who feared domination by the Na'ibs of Massawa, soon hastened to ally themselves with the Tigray.

As the Tigray serfs had found unity in a common desire for freedom, so now the chiefs and *shumagulle* united in defence of their privileges. Their need for influential allies was urgent and it was only to be expected that they should turn to the Nationalists for help. At a time when the British press was drawing attention to their lack of Moslem support, the Nationalists were only too ready to welcome Moslem recruits and give them the assurances they demanded.

It is improbable that Ibrahim Sultan and his followers had at first any purpose beyond securing the emancipation of the Tigray serfs and winning themselves rank and authority. Now, however, they had cause to fear that, unless the Nationalists were effectively opposed, Eritrea might pass by default to Ethiopia, which in that event would then be bound to honour the undertakings the chiefs and *shumagulle* had received from the Nationalists.

It might be supposed that Ibrahim Sultan would at this stage have sought union with the Separatists. Though founded, organized, and led by Christian Abyssinians, the Separatist movement had been supported by the Moslem Jiberti and also by the large group of Saho tribes. The Jiberti and Saho needed allies to defend their interests, but neither group felt comfortable in an organization where, as Moslems, they were the junior partners; and among the more sophisticated Jiberti there had for some time been vague chatter about breaking away and allying themselves with their fellow Moslems elsewhere. With the emergence of the Tigray movement some form of Moslem union at last became practicable. Any thoughts which Ibrahim Sultan might have had of uniting with the Separatists was forestalled by the Jiberti and Saho deserting the Separatists to join their fellow Moslems in the west.

Eritrea

Their decision to do so was precipitated by a brief rapprochement between the Christian Separatists and the Unionist Party, which was brought about by their common grief and indignation over the Sudanese incident in August. During October 1946 the leaders of the two movements informed the Administration of their joint desire that Eritrea should be an autonomous state within the framework of the Ethiopian Empire. The agreement was shortlived and soon forgotten, but it showed that, left to themselves, Separatist and Nationalist were capable of reasonable compromise. Had Colonel Negga Haile Selassie not been absent in Addis Ababa at the time, it is unlikely that any discussions would have been held or any agreement reached. On his return in November Gebremaskal Woldu, the Secretary General of the Unionist Party and the chief advocate of the agreement, suddenly 'resigned' and, simultaneously, the Unionist Party abruptly repudiated it. The party leaders were no longer free agents. They had become servants of the Ethiopian Government.

In the meantime Ibrahim Sultan invited all Moslem communities to send representatives to a meeting at Keren on 4 December to consider the question of Eritrea's future. At the meeting the representatives agreed to form a Moslem League with Seyid Bubakr bin Othman Al Mirghani, the head of the Eritrean branch of the Tariqa Khatmia, as President, and Ibrahim Sultan as Secretary General. Discussion on the territory's future was deferred to a further meeting which was to be held on 21 January 1947. During the interval between the two meetings it became apparent that, though they were all firmly opposed to union with Ethiopia, opinion amongst the various Moslem groups was otherwise divided. The Tigray and Baria favoured some form of British administration as the best insurance of their interests. The few chiefs and *shumagulle* of the Tigray tribes who had entered the League had no reason to favour a British régime. The Jiberti and townsfolk of Massawa, who at this time were suffering from acute unemployment, looked back with frank regret to the golden days of the Italian régime. The Saho grumbled that the British had done nothing to restrain Abyssinian aggression, and the Kunama complained that they had never suffered such damage and injury as during the British Occupation. And, finally, the Danakil, who felt aggrieved that the British had done nothing to save their traditional though unofficial leader Muhammad Yahya, the Sultan of Aussa, from arrest by the Ethiopians during 1944 and subsequent death in Addis Ababa, spoke quite openly in favour of an Italian régime.

And so while the Tigray serfs favoured some form of British

The Growth of Political Consciousness, 1941–7

régime, the others did not. Some hankered after a restoration of Italian authority, though at this stage it was doubted whether Italy, having renounced all right and title to her colonies, could return to Eritrea. The majority vaguely favoured independence after a limited period of international trusteeship. Partition found no supporters. The Bani Amir clans opposed it believing the Sudan Government would favour the Hadendowa; and the Saho, Danakil, Samhar, and Jiberti followed suit, because it would include them within Ethiopia. In the event it was unanimously resolved that 'the territorial unity of Eritrea, as it was before 1935, be maintained' since the League 'does not accept nor adhere to any decision aiming to partition Eritrea'. The resolution added 'that the independence of Eritrea should be recognized or, in case this is held to be impossible, . . . that she should be placed under an international trusteeship . . . for ten years . . . with British control or such control as may be directed by the Trusteeship Council of the U.N.O.'

The qualified reference to British trusteeship in the declaration was sufficient to convince the Unionists that the League was a creature of the Administration. Though they had themselves openly exploited the Coptic Church to their own political advantage, the Unionists now addressed petitions to the Administration demanding the League's immediate dissolution on the ground that simple folk had been induced to join it for religious reasons alone. Moslems were invited to remember that they and the Christian Eritreans were brothers, and begged not to split the country. Bribes were offered to Moslem leaders to resign from the League. At the same time Colonel Negga Haile Selassie found time to tour the Moslem areas and make personal contact with most of the chiefs and *shumagulle* of the Tigray tribes.

The Unionists were also naturally concerned to dissuade the Separatists from making common cause with the League. In June 1947 Ras Seyum was suddenly released from detention in Addis Ababa and appointed Governor General of the Tigrai as a gesture to placate his sympathizers in Eritrea. Pro-Ethiopian demonstrations and processions were organized in every part of the country. The Emperor Haile Selassie's daughter, Princess Tenange Worq and her husband Bitwoded Andargachew, visiting Eritrea 'for health reasons', carried out an elaborate tour of the territory in February 1947. Everything possible was done to impress the Separatists with the inevitability of union with Ethiopia.

This display of anxious energy achieved nothing. In March the Separatists reconstituted themselves as an exclusively Christian organization named the Liberal Progressive Party and coupled sup-

Eritrea

port for the Moslem League's declaration with a claim for the 'restoration' of the Tigrai to Eritrea. The opposition to Unionism was now substantial and firm. In despair some of the younger Unionists in Asmara turned to terrorism, carrying out a number of attacks with hand-grenades and explosives against Moslem League and Liberal Progressive personalities.

This sudden outbreak of violence drew attention to the completeness with which Eritrean unity had been shattered. Except for the few Christian Liberal Progressives ranged alongside the Moslem League and a handful of Moslem renegades in the Unionist Party, the Eritreans had rallied under their rival religious banners and now stood divided against one another in opposing Moslem and Christian factions.

ITALIAN INTERVENTION

The Italian population made an invaluable contribution to the welfare of Eritrea during the Occupation. Without its Italian staff, the Administration could not have functioned; without skilled Italian labour, the British and American war projects could never have been undertaken; without Italian industrial and agricultural enterprise, the Eritrean economy would have collapsed; and without the Italian example of disciplined behaviour, the Eritrean population might well have reacted more dangerously to the stresses and strains imposed upon it. It was, therefore, paradoxical that the Italians, who did so much to ease the burden of British responsibility, should lose so much from British rule.

The Italians were, of course, the victims of circumstances. To live tolerably well they had both to work and to submit to, and in some measure collaborate with, British authority. If they were either workless or unco-operative they risked internment in India, South Africa, or the Middle East. The end of hostilities in 1945 released them from further fear of internment; and, as contact with Italy was re-established, it released them also from the hopeless sense of dependence on British authority which wartime isolation had bred. Gradually they became aware of the price they had had to pay for defeat; of what they had lost in prestige, social and political influence, and economic well-being. What probably hurt them most was the sudden and disagreeable change in the Eritreans' attitude towards themselves. They had been accustomed to respect and sometimes to personal affection and loyalty. They found it difficult to understand that, once they had relinquished power to British hands, the artificial façade of Eritrean respect and loyalty was bound to disintegrate. They found it easier to believe that British

The Growth of Political Consciousness, 1941–7

policy was deliberately designed to bring them into contempt. Their suspicions were probably first aroused by the sudden abandonment of fraternization early in 1942. Whatever the merits of this change in policy, which was arbitrarily ordered by British GHQ Middle East, it was singularly inopportune, coming at a time when the Americans engaged on war projects were cultivating the friendliest relations with the local Italian population. British aloofness was also coloured by an attitude of patronizing contempt for Italian methods and, indeed, for the Italians themselves, once social contact between British and Italians had ceased. It was natural that the Italians should see in this a deliberate attempt to undermine Eritrean respect for themselves.

The Italians also believed that the British were deliberately eradicating all Italian influence from Eritrea. The dismissal of Italian officials, the gradual exclusion of Italian administrative and judicial officials from dealings with Eritreans, the abandonment of Italian in Eritrean schools, and the various modifications of the Italian system of government seemed as clearly directed against Italian political influence as the removal of the official colour bar was designed to undermine the Italians' social position. It was also believed that the British had engineered the depression which struck Eritrea after 1945 as a means of squeezing the Italians out of the country. It was argued that Eritrea had a wealth of natural resources which Italian genius could have developed, had it not been for deliberate British interference. As it was the British had requisitioned the plant and equipment essential for development; they had crippled the skilled labour force by shipping thousands of Italians overseas; they had deprived Eritrea of its most valuable agricultural asset by abandoning cotton production; they had paralysed the one industry which might have revolutionized the territory's economy by restricting prospecting for gold; and they had made any large-scale development impossible by restricting the freedom of the banks to issue loans.

A growing Anglophobia was aggravated by apparent inconsistencies in the British approach to the question of Fascism. During the war years care had been taken to soft-pedal criticism of Fascism; and even when an anti-Fascist organization, the National Anti-Fascist Union, had been set up in 1942, the Administration had remained aloof from it. It was, however, difficult to justify so moderate an attitude once the war was over and the Italian Government itself was denouncing Fascism. And so, with the end of the war, there was an abrupt change in the British attitude. Fascism was openly and vigorously attacked; and symbols or reminders of Fascism such as street names, inscriptions, and emblems were changed or destroyed.

Eritrea

The mood of the Italians in Eritrea was very different from that of their compatriots in Italy. In Italy suffering and fear had bred revulsion against Fascism and relief at its collapse. In Eritrea the Italians had been spectators of the drama, not actors in it. Military defeat brought with it a sense of bitter humiliation, not relief. It brought also a mood of defiant patriotism which, temporarily, encouraged a resurgence of Fascist feeling. And so, when they needed the most delicate handling, the Italians in Eritrea found themselves treated with unexpected roughness.

It was thus in a mood of resentful hostility to the Administration that the Italians turned their attention to the problem of Eritrea's future. Though several Italian political parties had emerged by 1946, it was soon evident that Monarchists, Republicans, Christian Democrats, Socialists, and Communists all hoped to see the Italian tricolour fly again in Eritrea. They had no serious objection to some form of international trusteeship with a European administering authority, so long as this was not British. What they most dreaded was union with, as they believed, an uncivilized and vengeful Ethiopia, or partition, which would leave the bulk of the Italian population under Ethiopian rule. They did not seriously believe Ethiopian claims would be realized. Their real fear was of partition, for which they suspected the British had been working, first, by encouraging the Unionists on the Plateau and the Moslem League in the Lowlands and, secondly, by introducing Arabic and Tigrinya into the schools.

Though they had reason for anxiety during the period of the London and Paris Conferences, the Italians did nothing to win over the many Moslems who might at that time have responded to an Italian approach. By failing to do so they lost their opportunity, for Eritrean political allegiances were rapidly taking durable form. Many believed that defeated Italy was debarred from recovering her lost territories; many underestimated the political importance of Eritrean opinion; but probably most Italians did nothing because, by force of habit, they were awaiting instructions from Rome.

Before 1946 Italian metropolitan opinion had been more concerned with the fate of Istria, Trieste, Briga, and Tenda than that of the remote colonies. But during 1946 propaganda from the Ministry of the Colonies, which had nothing else to do, and the publication of the *Voice of Africa*, a weekly newspaper representing the views of a vociferous group of 'colonial refugees', brought the colonial problem to a more general public notice and interest in it quickly spread. 'Colonial Conferences' were held at Rome; the press devoted increasing space to the colonial question and, in time, there was a

The Growth of Political Consciousness, 1941–7

unanimous demand throughout Italy for the restoration of Eritrea and the other colonies.

The Italian argument was that, by reason of her past achievements and peculiar experience, Italy had a right to complete her uncompleted mission of guiding Eritrea (and the other colonies) to full maturity. Also it was claimed that the British had deliberately impoverished the territory and promoted communal strife as part and parcel of a policy of *divide et impera*. Italian arguments were couched in the familiar jargon of the times and the peculiarly British vice of 'colonialism' was oddly contrasted with what was described as Italy's 'civilizing mission' in Africa.

Though the terms of the Peace Treaty had foreshadowed the arrival of 'commissions of investigation' in the former Italian colonies 'to ascertain the views of the local population', the Italians remained inactive in Eritrea until March 1947, when an Eritrean Old Soldiers' Association suddenly came into being. Though ostensibly a non-political organization, it was known that it had been formed, and was controlled, by a small group of Italians to provide cover for a pro-Italian party. There were thousands of Eritrean ex-soldiers with claims to pay which they had never received; there were others entitled to gratuities and pensions which were as yet unpaid. It was made known that one of the Association's primary objects would be to press the Italian Government to honour its obligations; and that the Italian Government was unlikely to accept claims from outside the Association. In July it was announced that the Italian Government intended to send a Commission to Eritrea to examine the claims of Eritrean ex-soldiers; simultaneously the Association declared itself in favour of an Italian trusteeship and added the prefix 'Pro-Italy' to its title.

The Unionist Party and Moslem League had watched these developments with some anxiety. As soon as the Association showed itself in its true colours both parties demanded its dissolution on the grounds that it was not formally registered as a political organization. The argument was trivial, for all the Association had to do to regularize its position was to apply for the permission it needed. Nevertheless the Administration ordered its dissolution in apparent response to the protests of the Unionist Party and Moslem League. Immediately the sponsors of the Association applied for permission to form a 'Pro-Italy' Party. The protests which followed from the Unionists and Moslem League so preoccupied the Administration that approval was not given until a month later; and, even so, it was conditional on the party's headquarters being at Asmara and not, as it had asked, at Keren and also on Italians being excluded from its membership. The formation of the other parties had been approved without delay and without conditions. The Italians could scarcely be blamed for suspecting the Administration of calculated partiality.

The Administration's clumsy handling of this affair was unfortunate, since it provided the Italians with a legitimate grievance and a plausible explanation for the subsequent failure of the Pro-Italy Party. In fact this never had any hope of substantial support once the majority of Moslems had committed themselves to the League. In the event it enrolled some Jiberti and Danakil, a few Saho and Belain with grievances against the Administration, a handful of *shumagulle* from the Tigray tribes, a number of unemployed in Massawa, and a medley of ex-soldiers with claims on the Italian Government. Without covert Italian direction and funds the party could never have survived. As a political force it was negligible.

IV
THE DISPOSAL OF ERITREA
The Problem

The problem of Eritrea's disposal was complicated by the diversity of its inhabitants and its historical links with Ethiopia and Italy. There were two possible solutions. It could become independent either immediately or after a period of trusteeship; or it could be united partially or wholly with Ethiopia. Neither alternative was free of serious objection.

The Moslem League and Liberal Progressive Party, though demanding independence, had agreed to a trusteeship for ten years, should Eritrea be considered too backward to become independent immediately, and, in such an event, had expressed their preference for a British administering authority. They may have done so to flatter the British, but their preference was not unreasonable. Healthy development must depend on continuity of government, and policies which have been initiated being allowed to run their full course. Since development in Eritrea had been inspired by British teaching and guided by British leadership, any change of government would be damaging. Changing horses unnecessarily in midstream would be time-wasting and hazardous.

There were, however, two serious objections to independence, whether immediate or deferred. Ethiopia's claims and the feelings of the great mass of Eritrea's Christian Abyssinians could not be ignored. Ethiopian acquiescence in an independent Eritrea was out of the question; both because post-war Ethiopia was hungry for new territories, and because experience had taught her that, unless she had the key to her own front door, she would never be secure. Given Ethiopian encouragement and aid, the Eritrean Abyssinians might well revolt and overthrow the Government of an independent Eritrea, which would be unlikely to have much support outside the Moslem tribes. Even if Ethiopia and the Eritrean Abyssinians acquiesced in a trusteeship, Eritrea had no better prospect of survival as an independent state, once this had ended, than if it obtained immediate independence.

Few powers could be expected to undertake so irksome, expensive, and purposeless a task. Italy alone had an interest in doing so for reasons of national prestige. But of all solutions the resuscitation of

Eritrea

Italian authority was the least practical. Ethiopia could be counted upon to resist it by every possible means. Moreover, in such an event, the Tigray Moslems might well unite with the Abyssinians. Whatever arguments Italian apologists might advance in favour of an Italian trusteeship, the fact remained that since Italy would be actively opposed by at least 75 per cent. of the population, she could never expect to govern effectively.

There were also economic objections to independence. Eritrea was a poor country, where elaborate administrative and public services had been subsidized by Italian and British grants-in-aid. It was arguable that these services were unduly elaborate and that, if they were simplified, Eritrea might be able to stand on its own feet. Certainly simplification might balance budgets; but if Eritrea's wasting economic assets were to be preserved and exploited, standards needed to be improved rather than lowered. Land hunger, soil erosion, and overstocking would not be solved by cutting down technical services. None of the capital needed for development would be attracted from abroad unless standards of government were reasonably good.

The union of Eritrea with Ethiopia offered a more practical solution to the problem. Ethiopia needed Eritrea's ports and industrial installations for her own development. She had the resources to finance Eritrean development and the land to absorb Eritrea's surplus population and livestock. Eritrea was the economic complement to Ethiopia, and economically the union of the two countries was logical and rational; it offered Eritrea the only alternative to parasitism or bankruptcy.

There was, however, the serious objection that the Moslem half of the population was bitterly opposed to it. To ignore their feelings would be dangerous. There was much to be said for the division of the territory into Christian and Moslem regions, whereby the Plateau would be included within Ethiopia, and the Christian Abyssinians would have what they wanted without involving more than the Moslem Jiberti in unwilling subjection to Ethiopian rule. But that would have been its sole merit. Road and rail communications were centred on Asmara; the port of Massawa and Asmara were economically interdependent; and indeed the whole of eastern Eritrea had become an economic appendage of the Plateau.

The same arguments did not apply to the remaining three-fifths of the Moslem population in western Eritrea. There were economic links between them and the Plateau which could only be disrupted at the cost of some disturbance to the economic life of both regions. But the degree and extent of disturbance were unlikely to be so

The Disposal of Eritrea

serious as to outweigh the political advantages of partition. The objection here was political, not economic. Independence for so small and impoverished a region was out of the question. The only practical alternative was its union with the Sudan; but a solution on these lines would find no support in Eritrea and, because of the bitter feud between the Bani Amir and Hadendowa, least of all from the Tigray tribes who would be incorporated in the Sudan.

An alternative compromise was federal union with Ethiopia. It would give Eritrea the economic and, to some extent, financial benefits of full union without the disadvantage of Ethiopian interference in its domestic affairs. The difficulty was that Ethiopia would not favour it, and without Ethiopian consent no federation could survive. Ethiopia's Empire had been preserved by the concentration of power and authority in its central Government. To admit the principle of federation in the case of Eritrea might well spark off secessionist movements in other provinces where the direct control of the central Government was unwelcome.

Viewed in its parochial setting the problem was complex enough; set against the background of international politics it was to become even more complicated.

THE FAILURE OF THE FOUR POWERS TO RESOLVE THE PROBLEM

The foreign ministers of the 'Big Four' first met to draft the Italian Peace Treaty in September 1945, but it was not until 10 February 1947 that they finally agreed upon the terms of a treaty, which subsequently came into force on 15 September of the same year. The protracted course of the negotiations was largely explained by their differences over the colonial question. Even so these had not been resolved. The Treaty provided that Italy's colonies should be jointly disposed of by the Soviet Union, the United Kingdom, the United States, and France within one year of its coming into force,[1] but that

> If with respect to any of these territories the Four Powers are unable to agree upon their disposal within one year from the coming into force of the Treaty of Peace with Italy, the matter shall be referred to the General Assembly of the United Nations for a recommendation, and the Four Powers agree to accept the recommendation, and to take appropriate measures for giving effect to it.[2]

Had the unity of the Four Powers survived their victory, they might well have resolved the problem within the short time at their disposal, but a widening gulf was already dividing East from West.

[1] United Nations, *Treaty Series*, vol. 49, p. 139.   [2] Ibid. p. 215.

Eritrea

Russia's interference in Greece, Germany, Yugoslavia, and Eastern Europe had so alarmed the West that its statesmen were becoming obsessed with the threat from the East and preoccupied with devising the means of countering it.

It might be supposed that such a remote, small, and poor territory as Eritrea would offer little to excite the interest or cupidity of the great powers. Had they been required to dispose of Eritrea alone this might have been so. But the Eritrean problem was part of the larger problem embracing Somalia, Cyrenaica, and Tripolitania. Though largely desert and sparsely inhabited, Cyrenaica and Tripolitania had, by the accident of geography, acquired an exceptional strategic value. Nowhere in the Eastern Mediterranean are there better sites for air bases than on the flat expanse of the Libyan littoral. From the Western point of view, control or influence over the region was a necessity.

Differences in tradition and experience inclined each of the Western powers to visualize different means to this end. The British believed that the defence and political stability of the Middle East depended on the maintenance of their own influence, and saw the problem as one of finding a compromise between emergent nationalisms and British authority. In North Africa they first advocated immediate independence for Libya, but later agreed to an Italian trusteeship in Tripolitania, provided that they themselves obtained a trusteeship in Cyrenaica. They proposed that Somalia should be united with the other Somali territories held by Britain, France, and Ethiopia to form a United Somaliland which would be granted independence after a suitable period of United Nations trusteeship, preferably with a British administering authority; and in the case of Eritrea they favoured some form of partition, and suggested that either the Big Four or the United Nations Trusteeship Council should examine the advisability of ceding part of Eritrea to Ethiopia.

The French viewed the British proposals with misgiving. Though each was designed to preserve British influence, each favoured local nationalisms and thereby had disagreeable implications for colonial régimes elsewhere. An independent Libya would offer a serious threat to the French position in North Africa; a United Somaliland would destroy it in East Africa. The French were still smarting from the loss of their mandated territories in the Levant and believed that Western interests would be best served by the containment rather than encouragement of capricious Middle Eastern and African nationalist movements. Because of this they proposed that each territory should become an international trust and that Italy should be trustee. They did, however, stipulate that the Fezzan province of

84

The Disposal of Eritrea

Tripolitania, which was already in French military occupation, should be ceded to France, and that Ethiopia should be given access to the Red Sea by way of the Eritrean port of Assab.

The Americans were variously influenced by their distaste for 'colonialism' and their peculiar sensitivity to the Russian threat. At first they turned to Article 81 of the United Nations Charter (which permits the United Nations as such to administer trust territories) and proposed that each territory should be placed under a collective trusteeship,[3] that Ethiopia should be given an outlet to the sea at Assab, and that Libya and Eritrea should be granted independence after ten years. The trusteeship in Somalia was to be of indefinite duration. Molotov, the Russian Foreign Minister, rejected these somewhat idealistic proposals as impracticable. The Americans then veered round in support of the French proposals, with, however, the proviso that the trusteeships in Libya and Eritrea should be of a prescribed duration; a *volte face* which Mr. Byrnes, the American Secretary of State, explained as being made in the interest of bringing about agreement. It was, however, also brought about by American anxiety at the spread of Communism in Italy, and Washington's fears that collective trusteeships in Africa might jeopardize the chances of American trusteeships in the Pacific.

The Russians were cynically opportunist. At first they proposed quite simply that the spoils of war should be divided between the victors. They demanded a trusteeship in Tripolitania for themselves, and suggested that the United States and Britain should have trusteeships in the other territories. Then, as international attention turned to the conflict between left and right wing factions in Italy, as a prelude to the elections which were due to be held in April 1948, they sought to win Italian favour by falling into line with the French and Americans. Though the three other powers were now in general agreement on Italian trusteeship, the British were not prepared to give way, if for no other reason because they were bound to honour Mr. (now Sir Anthony) Eden's undertaking, in the House of Commons on 8 January 1942, that the Sanussi of Cyrenaica should never again be subjected to Italian rule.[4] Largely because of British dissent, the attempt to grant Italy trusteeships over her former colonies failed; and since no agreement was possible, the Peace Treaty was, as we have seen, drafted with the object of giving the Four Powers a further and last chance of resolving the problem. Further discussions

---

[3] The United States proposal was that a 'neutral' administrator, responsible to the Trusteeship Council, should be given executive control in each territory; and that he should be assisted by an Advisory Committee comprising representatives of the Big Four, Italy, and two residents of the territory.

[4] H. C. Deb. vol. 377, col. 78.

Eritrea

resulted in agreement to dispatch a Commission of Investigation to the territories to report on conditions within them and on the wishes of their inhabitants.[5]

Though the Commission's task might well have kept a disinterested team of experts fully occupied for a year in Eritrea, it only remained in the territory from 12 November 1947 until 3 January 1948. It was composed of four national delegations. With the exception of Mr. F. E. Stafford, the head of the British delegation, who as a member of the Colonial Service had served in Africa and had more recently been adviser to the Ethiopian Government, no head of delegation had experience or knowledge of territories such as Eritrea. Mr. J. E. Utter, his American colleague, was a banker who had spent a few months in North Africa; M. Étienne Burin des Roziers, the head of the French delegation, was a professional diplomat who had only served in Western countries; Mr. A. F. Feodorov, the Russian, was a soldier who had recently come from Manchuria. Only the British and French delegates had advisers with African experience.

The Commission took some time to decide how it was to set about its task. Since its members had neither the technical knowledge nor time to make any direct investigation into the 'political, economic, and social conditions' obtaining in the territory, it had to inform itself from such sources as were available. Questionnaires were accordingly addressed to the British Administration and all political, social, and professional organizations were invited to submit their views. Within a comparatively short time the Commission's offices were congested with a mass of documents: reports by the Administration, treatises by the local organizations, and written records of the many interviews with their representatives. The Administration took care to express no views and to confine itself to statements of fact. The local organizations were more inclined to express opinions and to suit the facts to their arguments.

And so the staffs of the four delegations painstakingly sifted the many hundreds of documents before them for what would suit their arguments best. In committee and in full Commission precious time was frittered away in unrewarding discussion; each delegate quoting a different source to prove his point or challenge an argument. With such a variety of information at their disposal and no accepted

[5] 'The task of the Commission shall be to collect and supply the Deputies with the necessary data on the question of the disposal of the former Italian Colonies and to ascertain the views of the local population. . . . This shall include data regarding political, economic and social conditions in each colony, as well as the wishes and welfare of the inhabitants and the interests of peace and security' (*Four Power Commission Report*, App. 1).

The Disposal of Eritrea

means of testing its reliability, the delegates could not readily agree on what was a fact. The following extract from a letter from a member of the British delegation may be quoted as an example of the absurdity of much of the discussions.

We had a meeting of the Commission's Political and Social Committee [he wrote] and examined a draft chapter for the Commission's report on health which had been prepared by Klimov, the Russian. In it he paid somewhat extravagant tribute to the Italians and, as an instance of what they had done, referred to a large and splendidly equipped sanatorium they were supposed to have built, in a village not very far from Asmara. There is, of course, no such sanatorium and I said so. Klimov produced one of the many glossy-paged Fascist publications, which some Italian delegation has delivered here, and pointed to a paragraph in which there was mention of its existence. I explained that, for propaganda purposes, publications of this kind often recorded buildings or schemes as having come into being before even the planning had been completed. In any event I suggested that, if he and other members of the Committee doubted my word, they could without inconvenience go to the village and see for themselves if the sanatorium existed or not. Klimov refused the invitation. We were here, he said, to establish facts. It was a fact that this particular publication had stated that the Italians had built the sanatorium. Whether they had done so or not was immaterial. The fact had been established.

Though much time was wasted in argument of this kind, the Commission eventually agreed on a report which, in three chapters, gave a reasonably comprehensive and accurate account of 'political, social, and economic conditions' in the territory.

There was even less prospect of agreement when they turned to the task of ascertaining the wishes of Eritrea's inhabitants. Each political party claimed the support of the overwhelming majority of the population. How was the Commission to find out the truth? The difficulty was that there was no tried or accepted method of consulting the population acceptable to the Commission. The population's official spokesmen were the chiefs and Advisory Council members but, being appointed by the Administration, their views would be suspect. Anything in the nature of a plebiscite would be impracticable. A large part of the population was nomadic and, apart from other difficulties, there would be no time to publicize details of procedure and carry out a registration of voters.

It was a problem to which the Administration had already given much anxious thought. It was foreseen that the Commission would arrive with no plan, and that even if a plan were quickly hatched there would be no time to implement it. In the absence of some arrangement which would provide Eritreans with a reasonable oppor-

Eritrea

tunity of making their views known to the Commission, there was the danger that they would attempt to advertise their political allegiance by resorting to disorder. The Administration could not remain indifferent to such an eventuality and, at the risk of a possible rebuff, it took the step of implementing a plan of its own in advance of the Commission's arrival.

Of the various alternative methods of consultation suggested, it favoured an arrangement whereby each family group or clan would elect a representative, and the representatives from each district would then express their views individually to the Commission. The Administration had records of the size of each clan and family, and since almost all had by this time joined one of the political parties, it was thought that by recording their allegiances and population figures the Commission would be able to arrive at a reasonably precise estimate of the support each party commanded. Though the election of representatives posed a number of questions, they were speedily overcome; and before the Commission's arrival every clan and family had elected a representative. In all 3,336 representatives.

The British and Americans were prepared to accept the Administration's arrangements. The Russians argued that they only had the Administration's word that the representatives had in fact been elected. The French claimed that the Commission's task was to discover what the population desired and not what the strength of each party was. The Russians questioned the accuracy of the Administration's population figures. The French argued that in any event they had no value since, in each case, they were given for a whole community and did not indicate how many individuals had voted for the successful candidate. Nevertheless, in the absence of any alternative, the Russians and French had to accept the Administration's arrangements, though in doing so they insisted on two provisos. First, each representative was to be asked what he and his supporters desired and not what party they favoured; and, secondly, each was to state how many persons he represented, and his claim was to be recorded and not the population figures provided by the Administration.

In spite of the first Franco-Russian proviso, the desires expressed by the representatives followed the various party lines so clearly that it was easier to group them by party than by the actual phrases they employed. The records of the Commission showed that according to their 'claims', the Unionist representatives had the support of 44·8 per cent. of the population; the Moslem League representatives 40·5 per cent.; the Liberal Progressives 4·4 per cent.; the

The Disposal of Eritrea

Pro-Italy Party 9·2 per cent.; and an insignificant Moslem splinter group, the National Party (which favoured any kind of British administration) 1·1 per cent.[6]

The geographical incidence of the support claimed by each group of representatives was as had been expected. On the Plateau (which for this purpose included the Saho tribal area) 71·1 per cent. of the population was 'claimed' as favouring union with Ethiopia as against only 14·9 per cent. claimed by those who favoured the Moslem League proposals. Elsewhere the latter claimed 71·6 per cent. of the population as against only 12·9 per cent. claimed as supporting union with Ethiopia.[7]

In short the investigations confirmed that, with the exception of the Moslem League and Unionist Party, no political organization had any valid following, and that the population divided its support between them largely in terms of geography and religion.

The French and Russian delegations could not be expected to welcome so unequivocal a denial of Italian pretensions. Thereafter they set out to discredit the inquiry. They compared the number of supporters claimed by the representatives with the official population figures (the authenticity of which they had previously questioned), and, finding the total claimed to be greatly in excess of the official figures, argued that they must be exaggerated and, therefore, meaningless. They cast doubts on the validity of the representatives, arguing that the methods of election said to have been employed were remote from normal democratic practice. They insisted that most representatives had shown little understanding of the official aims of the political parties they supported. It was pointed out, for example, that, on being questioned, many Moslem League tribal representatives had admitted either that they had not known the League's aims or that they had expressed views at variance with them. Unionist representatives were criticized for their parrot-like repetition of party slogans, which, it was argued, betrayed ignorance of Unionist aims.

The Commission's report consequently revealed a sharp difference of opinion between the British and Americans on the one hand and the Russians and French on the other. In an agreed draft the former recorded their view that

it is obvious that the country is split into two camps and that political thought in each is conditioned in the main by religious belief. Furthermore, these two dominant religious creeds are congregated, one in the Christian highlands and the other in the Moslem lowlands and plains.

---

[6] *Four Power Commission Report*, p. 98.   [7] Ibid. p. 102.

Eritrea

The Christian inhabitants of the three plateau provinces, apart from an important minority, are strongly in favour of unconditional union with Ethiopia. . . .

The Moslem areas of the lowlands and the Western Plain are in favour of eventual independence but generally agree that an interim period under U.N. control will be necessary. . . . Preference is given for the U.K. to be the trustee.[8]

The Russians and French expressed their views in similar terms but in separate drafts. The Russians stated that

> XI. There is no group of representatives having a complete majority of the total number of representatives. . . . An important factor which affected the number of representatives from the Pro-Italy party was that the formation of this party was only authorised just before the arrival of the Commission. . . .
> XII. It was found that . . . the representatives were backward people. . . .
> XIII. As a result of the investigation an impression was gained that the population will accept the decision of the Big Four even if it does not coincide with the opinions expressed by the representatives.[9]

The French endorsed their view remarking that

'The general impression left by conversations with a large number of persons belonging to all the parties is that they would accept the decision of the Four Powers, even if it were contrary to the wishes expressed by their parties.'[10]

The Council of Foreign Ministers met to examine the Commission's report in September 1948. Their discussions revealed the differences which a divided report had foreshadowed. The British shelved their previous proposals and now proposed that Eritrea should be placed under an Ethiopian administration for ten years; as a safeguard for the Italian minority and Moslems they also proposed that an advisory council should be set up to assist the Administration, which would comprise representatives of Italy, a Moslem state, and non-colonial Powers. The Americans proposed the immediate cession of Dankalia and of the two Plateau divisions of the Serai and Akelli Guzai to Ethiopia, leaving the fate of the remainder of the territory to be decided twelve months later. The French, not unexpectedly, stood firm in favour of an Italian trusteeship, though they were ready to concede Ethiopia an outlet to the Red Sea through Assab. And, finally, the Russians, after first renewing their former proposals for an Italian trusteeship, suddenly startled the others by coming out in favour of a collective international trusteeship, the very proposal which they had rejected as impracticable

---

[8] *Four Power Commission Report*, p. 96.   [9] Ibid. pp. 107–8.   [10] Ibid. p. 105.

The Disposal of Eritrea

when it had first been made by the Americans. No agreement was possible. On 15 September the Four Powers washed their hands of the problem and referred it to the United Nations.

The Commission's visit and the Four Powers' handling of the problem did not ease the Administration's task. A colonial government's authority is largely accepted because, in the eyes of the subject people, it is supreme, unchallengeable, and there is no alternative to it. Set against the background of the Four Powers the Administration's stature no longer seemed supreme. Many representatives had been able to criticize the Administration to the Commission.

It was natural that Eritreans should transfer their interest from a moribund Administration to those who seemed likely to be their future governors, and that, in consequence, the influence of the political parties and their leaders should suddenly increase. Claimants to land, aspirants to appointments, and those in search of other favours now began to look to the political parties for support, and in a decreasing degree to the Administration. It was useful that the party agents, who were mostly townsmen, should become better acquainted with the bread-and-butter politics of the rural Eritrean; in other respects their intrusion into village and tribal affairs was deplorable. They sought popularity not justice. Their method of achieving it was not to allay but to arouse false hopes, futile ambitions, and dormant enmities. The prestige and popularity of the Administration were diminishing; the increase in the influence of the political leaders was only matched by their irresponsibility and increasing capacity to cause mischief.

This became apparent within two weeks of the Four Power Commission's departure when armed gangs of Christian Abyssinians or Shifta, as they were commonly known, began a series of attacks against Italian and Moslem life and property. They continued until the meeting of the foreign ministers of the Four Powers in September. Six Italians and fifteen Moslems were murdered. Five of the latter were tied up and beheaded with swords in the presence of their women and children. Italian farms and gold mines were raided and damaged. Large numbers of livestock belonging to the Moslem tribes in western Eritrea were looted. Rail and road transport was interrupted. The victims of these outrages were all either opposed to union with Ethiopia or connected with those who were. At the scene of many outrages the Shifta left letters declaring their loyalty to the Emperor Haile Selassie and threatening his enemies with death. At the same time Miss Sylvia Pankhurst's *New Times and Ethiopian News* was describing the Shifta as 'patriots' and the Ethiopian authorities

Eritrea

were openly granting them refuge in the Addi Abo district of the Tigrai. That the disturbances were inspired by the Unionist Party and, indeed, the Ethiopian Government itself was taken for granted throughout Eritrea.

It was simple terrorism, calculated to attract the attention of the Four Powers and influence their deliberations. The results of the Commission's inquiry had undoubtedly shocked the Unionist leaders, who, until then, had mostly believed that they were only opposed by a handful of ambitious Christian Abyssinian chiefs and a somewhat nebulous group of Moslems. They had been shocked also by the fact that Italy counted for very much more in the world than Ethiopia. They now attempted to impress the Four Powers and world opinion with Unionist strength and determination. Instead they revealed the hatred which was beginning to divide Eritrean from Eritrean.

THE DISPOSAL OF ERITREA BY THE UNITED NATIONS

It was vital to Eritrea that its political future should be settled without delay. Pressing economic problems such as urban unemployment and land hunger could not be tackled effectively by a temporary administration. Nor could it be expected to satisfy the younger and more sophisticated Eritrean's thirst for political advancement. Eritrea's interests demanded planned political, social, and economic development and the stability which would ensure an ordered progress. But until Eritrea's political future was known, no plans could be drawn up and no progress made. Indecision and delay not only arrested progress but encouraged conflict between Christian and Moslem and opened the door to strife and disorder. By their failure to reach any decision after three and a half years the Four Powers had already caused Eritrea serious injury. The United Nations was to cause even graver damage before making a decision a little more than two years later.

A significant consequence of the transfer of the problem to the United Nations was that Italy's power to influence a decision was greatly enhanced. The Ethiopians and Unionists had assumed that defeated Italy was implicitly debarred by the Peace Treaty from returning to her former colonies. They were deeply disturbed to find that was not so; nor were they soothed by the evident concern of some of the Four Powers to win Italian favour. But now Italy was in an even stronger position. As one of the United Nations she had a voice in the settlement of the problem, and, since she commanded the sympathy of the Latin American states, it was likely to be a decisive one.

The Disposal of Eritrea

Evidence of Italy's position of power was soon forthcoming in what was known as the Bevin–Sforza Agreement. In an attempt to get the problem settled Mr. Ernest Bevin, the British Foreign Secretary, had made obviously distasteful concessions to Count Sforza, the Italian Foreign Minister, in a joint set of proposals which were adopted by the First Committee of the General Assembly in May 1949. It was proposed that Italy should be granted trusteeships in Somalia and Tripolitania; that Cyrenaica should become independent after a period of British trusteeship; and that Eritrea should be partitioned between Ethiopia and the Sudan.[11] After the First Committee had adopted them, it seemed reasonably certain that the Bevin–Sforza proposals would be accepted by the Assembly. In the event an outburst of anti-Italian rioting in Tripolitania brought about a rapid change of opinion in New York before the First Committee's draft resolution was considered by the General Assembly on 17 May 1949. Voting took place on the proposal for each territory and then for the proposals as a whole. The Eritrean proposal was approved by 37 votes to 11, with 10 abstentions; the proposals as a whole were rejected by 37 votes to 14, with 7 abstentions. Eritrea was condemned to a further period of anxious uncertainty.

The defeat of the Bevin–Sforza proposals redirected Italian attention to Eritrea. It was now beyond question accepted that no amount of lobbying would enable Italy to recover her North African colonies; it seemed likely, however, that, in return for the withdrawal of her claims to them, she might win support over Eritrea and Somalia. Their fate was a matter of little direct interest to any country other than Ethiopia. The Arab and Asian states seemed ready to purchase independence for North Africa at the cost of an Italian trusteeship in Somalia, but it seemed unlikely that they would reject Ethiopian claims outright in favour of an Italian trusteeship in Eritrea. Italy's problem was to find a formula for Eritrea which would win international favour and yet ensure her a continuing influence in her oldest colony. She chose to do so by advocating the grant of immediate independence to Eritrea. It was the one solution which could be expected to win international support at the expense of Ethiopia.

The proposal had originated in an organization of Italian settlers and half-castes called the Italo-Eritrean Association, which had assumed covert control of the Pro-Italy Party after the Four Power

[11] 'That Eritrea, except for the Western Province, be incorporated into Ethiopia, under terms and conditions set forth below, to include the provision of appropriate guarantees for the protection of minorities . . . and that the Western Province be incorporated in the adjacent Sudan.' (*GAOR*, 3rd sess., pt. 2. 1st Committee, Annexes A/c. 1/466.)

Eritrea

Commission's departure. At that time they had hoped that, in their resentment at Britain's attitude during the Four Power discussions, the Moslems would come round to the Italian way of thinking. Though Moslem leaders such as Ibrahim Sultan were aware that an Italian alliance would bring them political support in New York and sorely needed financial assistance in Eritrea, they would not join in any demand for an Italian régime. If there was to be an alliance it would have to be on Moslem terms. The Moslem League had demanded independence after a period of trusteeship, preferably with a British administrative authority. The Italians could not be expected to agree to a British trusteeship; and since the Moslems would not countenance an Italian régime, the only possible common platform was that of independence.

Although they had been the first to ridicule the Moslem League's demands, the 'Italo-Eritrean' leaders began to see advantages in them, provided that independence came about as a result of Italian patronage. What they had in mind was a nominally independent Eritrea which would in practice be closely linked with Italy. As they saw it, Italy could take Eritrea under her wing by providing the financial and economic aid which it would need, and, if necessary, military protection as well. Within the territory it was envisaged that the Italians would enjoy Eritrean citizenship. Politically, they would hold the balance between the rival Moslem and Christian factions, and, because of their superior qualifications, they would control the machinery of government. Thinking of this kind was frequently expressed in discussion during the first months of 1949, and subsequently in the local Italian press.

In the event, the delegations of the Moslem League, Pro-Italy Party, and Italo-Eritrean Association met together in New York after the defeat of the Bevin–Sforza proposals and suddenly demanded immediate independence for Eritrea, with the full support of the Italian Government. On their return to Eritrea an approach was made to the Moslem League's old ally, the Liberal Progressive Party; and, within a short time, the three Eritrean political parties opposed to union with Eritrea had become formally federated as the Independence Bloc and pledged to the cause of immediate independence. Though the Bloc was formed hurriedly and without the knowledge or consent of the rank and file in the parties, the *fait accompli* was accepted without any overt opposition.

Claims that the Bloc had the support of the majority of the population were impressive; but it soon became apparent that Italy was leaving nothing to chance. Earlier in the year the Italian Government followed the example of the Ethiopians and appointed a Count

The Disposal of Eritrea

Di Gropello to Eritrea as liaison officer. He took little pains to conceal his activities; and it was soon known that he and the Italian agents working with him were disbursing very considerable sums of money in the cause of independence. Though the Unionists had used Ethiopian money to further their interests, they had never had the means to resort to bribery on so lavish a scale. However injudiciously expended, money could be expected to earn dividends among a poor and politically immature population. Many Christian communities living on the fringes of the Plateau, such as the Belain, deserted the Unionist Party; the few renegade Moslems with the Unionists now found excuses for abandoning them; and even among the staunchest Unionist communities the corrosive effect of Italian money became visible.

In September 1949 the Fourth Session of the General Assembly gave further consideration to the Italian colonial question. It decided that Libya should become independent immediately, and that Somalia should become independent after a ten-year period of Italian trusteeship. It also resolved on 21 November that a Commission should be set up

> to ascertain more fully the wishes and the best mean s of promoting the welfare of the inhabitants of Eritrea, to examine the question of the disposal of Eritrea and to prepare a report for the General Assembly, together with such proposal or proposals as it may deem appropriate for the solution of the problem of Eritrea.[12]

Subsequently, a Commission was appointed comprising representatives of Norway, Guatemala, South Africa, Pakistan, and Burma. The decisions on Libya and Somalia afforded the Unionists little comfort. They betrayed an unwelcome prejudice in favour of the principle of independence, which in the case of Somalia, where the population was at that time openly opposed to any form of Italian régime, revealed an unreasoning sympathy with Italy. With the Unionists losing ground in Eritrea there was every danger that the Commission would favour independence. The Bloc and its Italian patrons were jubilant; the local Italian press ridiculed Ethiopia's chances.

To understand what followed, it is as well to visualize what Unionist feelings were at this time. They saw the Bloc as an artificial organization, created out of Italian money to deceive world opinion with its specious demands for 'immediate independence': a transparent cover for indefinite dependence on Italy and subordination to the local Italian and half-caste minority. In Unionist eyes, the

[12] Resolution 289 (IV) (*GAOR*, 4th sess., Resolutions (A/1251), p. 11).

Eritreans in the Bloc were traitors who were selling out their country to Ethiopia's arch enemy.

In these circumstances it was natural that the Unionists should resort to violence. They had nothing to lose by it, and judging by events in Palestine and, more recently, in Tripolitania, everything to gain. The maxim that violence does not pay had been disproved, few Unionists doubted that it would pay the best and quickest dividends. Although there had been no serious disturbances since the disorders in 1948 after the Four Power Commission's departure, Unionist hotheads had carried out occasional acts of terrorism against their opponents with impunity. Soon after the Fourth Session of the General Assembly had ended, an organized campaign of terrorism and intimidation was launched against the Bloc. Between October 1949 and the arrival of the United Nations Commission in February 1950, 9 Italians, an Indian, a Greek, 3 Christian supporters of the Bloc, and 4 Moslem tribesmen were assassinated. Italian cafés in Asmara and Addi Ugri were attacked with rifle fire and hand-grenades; hand-grenades were thrown at Italian and Eritrean supporters of the Bloc in Asmara, Massawa, and Decamere; an open assault was made on the village of a district chief in the Akelli Guzai who supported the Bloc; Italian farms were raided and ransacked; and the livestock of Moslem tribesmen was looted. The climax came in February when, as the United Nations Commission was arriving, violent fighting broke out in Asmara between Moslems and Christians. It persisted for five days before order was restored, and resulted in a long casualty list of dead and wounded.

Terrorism and violence were supplemented by a campaign of threats against the Italians and the Eritrean supporters of the Bloc. In many cases the armed gangs of Christian Abyssinians or Shifta left letters or pamphlets at the scene of their outrages, threatening Italians with death if they supported the Bloc, and warning Eritreans that they and their families would suffer if they did not abandon it. The Coptic Church published a warning in the columns of *Ethiopia*, a Unionist publication which first appeared in 1948, that the Church would not grant facilities as regards baptism, marriage, burial, communion, and absolution to members of the Bloc or to their families. And Moslem Tigray tribesmen, who sometimes roamed across the Ethiopian frontier in search of grazing during the dry months of winter and spring, were now ejected by the Ethiopian authorities except in the few cases of those who were able to produce Unionist Party membership cards.

So violent and direct a campaign of intimidation earned its authors gratifying but not unexpected results. It made its profoundest

The Disposal of Eritrea

impression on those who had deserted, or who had contemplated deserting, the Unionist Party. They were now confronted with the choice between membership of the Bloc which, if lucrative, involved physical risk, and a safe-conduct back to the Unionist fold. Few hesitated to find suitable face-saving pretexts to desert the Bloc.

This was not the only blow to befall the Bloc. Within a few days of the Commission's arrival it was disrupted, losing more than half of its members as a result of serious splits in the Moslem League and Liberal Progressive Party. Although personal jealousies played a part, the cause of dissension was the severe distaste with which the anti-Italian wings in each party viewed the Bloc's close Italian connexions. At first the Bloc's alliance with the Italians had been accepted as a simple arrangement of convenience. But, in time, Italian exuberance and Unionist propaganda began to have their effect. What was the Bloc's attitude to the suggestion that Italians should acquire Eritrean citizenship? On what conditions would Italy provide an independent Eritrea with financial and technical assistance? On what terms were the Italians financing the Bloc? Questions such as these became dangerously charged with suspicion. The persuasive diplomacy of Ibrahim Sultan, who was now the Bloc's Secretary General, rode out several storms; but he was in no position to do more than purchase time by a process of evasion and procrastination. His ingenuity was, however, unequal to an impossible task.

The rebels in the two parties had little in common with each other but their Italophobia. Within the Moslem League the revolt was confined to western Eritrea. It was led by Sheikh 'Ali Musa Radai, the accepted, if unofficial, leader of a powerful group of Tigray tribes, which suspected Ibrahim Sultan's Italian connexions and opposed his tribal ambitions. They were equally opposed to Italian and Ethiopian pretensions. Their difficulty was that they had no positive convictions and, now that they were limited to western Eritrea, had to devise a policy in the same limited context. They were anxious for British support and, but for the Bani Amir–Hadendowa feud, might well have declared themselves in favour of western Eritrea's union with the Sudan. As it was, they fell back on the somewhat absurd demand that western Eritrea should acquire independence after a period of British trusteeship.

By deciding to go their own way the 'Moslem League of the Western Province', as the Moslem rebels now described themselves, turned their backs on the rebels in the Liberal Progressive Party. At heart, the latter still hankered after a greater Tigrai, but, with the independence movement in Italian hands and the Moslems of the west seeking to contract out of Eritrea, their leaders began to seek some form of accommodation with the Unionists. In their eyes union with Ethiopia was only objectionable because of Ethiopia's Shoan hegemony. If some form of union could be devised which would leave the management of Eritrea's affairs in Eritrean hands and preserve Eritrea's languages and customs, it would be incomparably more attractive than an Italian-sponsored independence. Thinking of this kind brought them round once more to what they termed 'conditional' or, in effect, federal union with Ethiopia. After a delegation led by Dejazmatch Abraha Tesemma had visited Addis Ababa and sounded the Ethiopian Government, the rebels constituted themselves as the 'Liberal Unionist' Party, pledged to bring about the 'conditional union' of Eritrea and Ethiopia.

These events left the Unionist Party in a much better position to withstand the scrutiny of the United Nations Commission. Behind the brave façade of the Independence Bloc, which was by this time claiming to be a federation of about a dozen parties and associations, there was now nothing but the old Pro-Italy Party and a rump of the Moslem League representing the Moslems of Asmara and Massawa, the Saho, Samhar, and Danakil, and the few Tigray who owed a personal loyalty to Ibrahim Sultan. The other organizations listed as members of the Bloc had few supporters outside their officials and paid agents. The Moslem League of the Western Province, though now the strongest party in western Eritrea, had no support elsewhere. Moreover, the formation of the Liberal Unionist Party had almost eliminated the only Christian Abyssinian opposition to the Ethiopian cause. Nor was this all. The Unionists came to a 'gentlemen's agreement' with the Moslem League of the Western Province to refrain from attacking each other and to co-operate in opposing the Bloc. The Unionists also agreed not to press Ethiopia's claims to the Western Province 'should the majority of the inhabitants of western Eritrea not desire union with Ethiopia'.

The United Nations Commission was required to 'ascertain more fully the wishes of the inhabitants of Eritrea, to examine the question of the disposal of Eritrea and to prepare a report for the General Assembly together with such proposal or proposals as it may deem appropriate for the solution of the problem of Eritrea'. Its terms of reference postulated an inquiry which would resolve the conflicting views of the Four Powers and determine, beyond reasonable doubt, what proportion of Eritreans favoured each solution and whether Eritrea was economically viable or not. A very much more thorough and precise inquiry was demanded than the Four Powers had been able to carry out. As it was, the United Nations Commission proved no more than a parody of the earlier Commission. It was composed

The Disposal of Eritrea

of two judges, Erling Qvale (Norway) and Aung Khine (Burma); two lawyers, Mian Zaud Din (Pakistan) and Carlos García Bauer (Guatemala); and a soldier, Major General F. H. Theron (South Africa). It only remained in the territory from 14 February to 6 April 1950 and, during that period, conducted its inquiry in indifferent imitation of the representatives of the Four Powers. The Administration was asked to furnish much the same information as it had to the previous Commission, and the representatives of the political parties and cultural, commercial, and technical organizations were invited once more to state their views. The Commission also left Asmara to visit some of the principal centres of the territory but it visited fewer places, and spent less time in doing so, than the Four Power Commission had done. In addition, whereas the latter had employed a definite system of inquiry to obtain the views of the population, the United Nations Commission did no more than carry out casual observations of rival political gatherings at each centre and address random questions to persons whose representative qualities it had no means of checking.

The work of the Commission was further handicapped by the open partiality of some of its members and by a clash of personalities within it. The Guatemalan and Pakistani delegates made no secret of their championship of independence; the Norwegian delegate displayed equal, though less obtrusive, partiality for the Ethiopian cause. The Guatemalan and Pakistani delegates, who were both professional lawyers, made it their practice to question Eritreans appearing before the Commission as though they were witnesses in a court of law. Representatives supporting the Independence Bloc were guided along with adroit inquiries and leading questions to make the very best of their case; those who opposed it were tripped up and trapped into admissions and contradictions in a most questionable form of cross-examination. The brusque, hectoring, and at times positively discourteous treatment which some of those appearing before the Commission received was widely commented on. So also were the several undignified wrangles and acrimonious exchanges which occurred in public between the representatives of Guatemala and Norway.

The sharp conflict of opinion within the Commission brought forth two separate reports and no less than three sets of proposals.[13] The Norwegian, South African, and Burmese delegates held that only a minority of the inhabitants favoured independence and that, as an independent entity, Eritrea would be economically unviable.

[13] *Report of the United Nations Commission for Eritrea* (General Assembly, Official Records: 5th sess., Supplement no. 8 (A/1285), 1950).

Eritrea

The Pakistani and Guatemalan delegates reported that terrorism and the Coptic Church's unwarrantable abuse of its powers had prevented any free expression of opinion; even so, they had no doubt that the great majority of the population wanted independence. And whereas the other three delegations agreed that Eritrea could not be economically viable, on the basis of data and statistics prepared by Dr. F. Van Biljoen, a qualified economist in the South African delegation, the Pakistani and Guatemalan delegates openly accused the Administration of preventing economic development as a means of furthering British hopes of partition.

The Norwegian, South African, and Burmese delegates, though in agreement that independence was neither practicable nor desired by the majority of Eritreans, parted company when they came to making positive proposals. The Norwegian delegate insisted that the union of Eritrea with Ethiopia was the only practicable solution, though he conceded that the Western Province should continue under a British administration for a period, after which its inhabitants should choose between union with Ethiopia or with the Sudan. His South African and Burmese colleagues viewed the problem as one of reconciling Eritrea's economic dependence on Ethiopia and the Ethiopian nationalism of the Plateau population, on the one hand, with Moslem and Italian suspicion of Ethiopia and Eritrean insularism on the other. The solution they proposed was that Eritrea should be a self-governing unit federated with Ethiopia under the sovereignty of the Ethiopian Crown. They envisaged an Eritrean Government with local legislative and executive autonomy, and a Federal Government responsible for defence, external affairs, interstate commerce, and communications.

The Pakistani and Guatemalan delegations argued that the large Moslem population and the important Italian minority could never be expected to acquiesce. Partition they rejected on the grounds that it would cause the country economic injury and was not, in any case, desired by the people. They conceded that a solution on federal lines merited consideration, but saw no reason to support it. Better, they argued, that Eritrea should become independent first, so that it would then be free to unite or federate with Ethiopia or remain independent, as it wished. They were, however, only prepared to concede independence after a ten-year period during which the United Nations, acting under the guidance of a Council comprising representatives of the United States, Ethiopia, Italy, a Moslem state, and a Latin American state, would hold the territory in trust and directly administer it.

Far from clarifying the findings of the Four Powers, the trivial

The Disposal of Eritrea

inquiry of the United Nations Commission added to them. And so, when it came to consider the Commission's report in September 1950, the General Assembly was no better informed as to what the inhabitants of Eritrea wanted, or the truth about Eritrea's economy, than it had been two years earlier. It was, however, in a better position to make a decision, the alternatives being narrowed down to the three solutions now put before it. Having no way of knowing which of the alternatives would serve Eritrea's interests best, it was bound to view the problem in its international context. From that point of view the federal solution proposed by the South African and Burmese delegations had much to commend it since it was a compromise between the extremes of union with Ethiopia and of independence. On 2 December 1950 the General Assembly adopted a resolution on the lines of the South African and Burmese recommendations by 46 votes to 10.[14]

By its resolution the General Assembly recommended that Eritrea should 'constitute an autonomous unit federated with Ethiopia under the sovereignty of the Ethiopian Crown'. The Eritrean Government was to have 'legislative, executive and judicial powers in the field of domestic affairs'. The jurisdiction of the Federal Government was to extend to 'defence, foreign affairs, currency and finance, foreign and interstate commerce and external and interstate communications including ports'. The jurisdiction of the Eritrean Government was to 'extend to all matters not vested in the Federal Government including the power to maintain the internal police, to levy taxes to meet the expenses of domestic functions and services, and to adopt its own budget'. An 'Imperial Federal Council composed of equal numbers of Ethiopian and Eritrean representatives' was to be set up. A single nationality was to 'prevail throughout the Federation'. There was to be a transition period not extending beyond 15 September 1952, during which the Eritrean Government was to be organized and an Eritrean constitution was to be prepared and put into effect. Meanwhile the British Administration was to retain responsibility for the conduct of Eritrean affairs, organize an Eritrean Administration, and convoke a representative Eritrean assembly. A United Nations Commissioner was to be appointed to draft an Eritrean constitution, which was to be approved by the Eritrean representative assembly and ratified by the Emperor of Ethiopia. With the appointment of Señor Eduardo Anze Matienzo of Bolivia as Commissioner on 14 December 1950 nothing more was left to be done but to implement the resolution.

[14] Resolution 390A (V) (*Final Report of the United Nations Commissioner in Eritrea* (*GAOR*, 7th sess., Supplement no. 15, A/2188), pp. 74–75).

Eritrea

It had taken five crowded years of argument, bargaining, and lobbying to resolve the Eritrean problem. The cost had to be paid by the Eritrean people. The promise offered by the modest progress realized during the first phase of the British Administration's life had never been fulfilled. In any territory emerging out of the colonial chrysalis the time comes when no further advance can be made until the political goal has been determined. In Eritrea the moment had come at the end of the war, but since then it had been left to the caprices of the Four Powers and United Nations; at different times being pushed to the brink of partition, union with Ethiopia, independence, and even Italian trusteeship. And so, during the first vital post-war years which witnessed such revolutionary progress in other colonial territories and, not least, in the neighbouring Sudan, little or no progress was realized in Eritrea.

This was as nothing to the damage and mischief resulting from Italian and Ethiopian interference. While international statesmen had debated Eritrea's future, the Ethiopians and Italians had organized and equipped rival Eritrean parties to combat each other in their own interests, and in doing so had not hesitated to exploit ancient enmities and arouse the most dangerous passions.

Without their support neither the Unionists nor the Bloc would have commanded a fraction of the following they now had. Nor would there have been any serious disorders in 1948 and 1949. Now, as a direct consequence of their interference, violence and disorder continued uninterruptedly, leaving a trail of death, injury, damage, and thirst for revenge until, at the time when the United Nations made its decision, large tracts of Eritrea were given over to anarchy. With the problem of Eritrea's future solved at last, it was widely believed that passions would die down and that order would be restored. The belief was illusory.

V
THE TRANSITION TO AUTONOMY IN PARTNERSHIP WITH ETHIOPIA
1951-2
THE PROBLEM OF SECURITY

The United Nations decision had to be put into effect before 15 September 1952. Since the United Nations Commissioner, Eduardo Anze Matienzo, did not arrive in Asmara until 9 February 1951 this meant that there were only nineteen months for all that it demanded and implied to be carried out. The Chief Administrator had to organize an Eritrean Government, induct Eritreans into it at all levels, convoke a representative assembly, and arrange for the transfer of power to Ethiopian and Eritrean authorities. The United Nations Commissioner had to draft an Eritrean constitution (after consulting the Administration, the Ethiopian Government, and the inhabitants of the country), submit it to the Eritrean representative assembly for acceptance, and then see to the setting up of an Eritrean Government.

But until the 'Shifta' who were at this time paralysing the country's government and economic life were brought under control, nothing could be done. After a cursory survey of the Eritrean scene, Sr. Anze Matienzo announced at a press conference on 1 May that he felt unable to continue until the situation had improved.

> I do not believe it advisable [he said] to begin these consultations at a time when the population, which desires peace and security above all else, is in danger. Furthermore, I do not think it proper that I should travel about the country flying the flag of the United Nations, over roads stained with the blood of people attacked by terrorists.[1]

To understand the problem, it is necessary to consider how the Shifta came to constitute so serious a menace.

'Rebel' or 'bandit' are the usual and perhaps best English renderings of the Ethiopic, but each has somewhat disreputable implications which the word Shifta does not necessarily imply. In the past, Ethiopia was continually disturbed by Shifta. The fierce, independent spirit of the people, their persistent vendettas, their thirst and

---
[1] *Progress Report of the United Nations Commissioner in Eritrea during 1951* (A/1959), p. 177.

recklessness for revenge, the wild and largely mountainous nature of their country, and, during the last hundred years, a plentiful supply of French and, later, Italian rifles were the ingredients of chronic lawlessness. Brigandage always offered comparatively easy prizes to any adventurer commanding an adequate following. The strongest could expect to blackmail a weak central authority into recognizing them as local rulers or, at least, into conniving at their illegalities. The majority could hope to live tolerably well by simple plunder, the extortion of 'protection money', or as mercenaries in the service of some feuding tribe or clan. Only petty thieves without influence had cause to fear punishment and disgrace.

Perhaps Italy's greatest contribution to Eritrea was that she maintained law and order in a country where they had previously been unknown. The Italian Government was an alien authority, its principal servants were, at best, only superficially acquainted with the country, and its prestige was shattered at the outset by humiliating defeat at Adowa. And yet a population which had been comparatively well armed was disarmed, pacified, and brought under control. Also the Shifta who had so long disturbed the peace were eliminated. The Italians always had a fair-sized army at their disposal, but it was not by military action alone that they achieved their purpose. While Italian military columns pursued their elusive quarries, punitive and precautionary measures were taken against the persons and property of those connected with the Shifta by blood or interest. Crops and livestock, and sometimes hostages, were seized against the surrender of Shifta; by way of punishment collective fines were levied, houses and crops were destroyed, and military garrisons were quartered in villages as a charge against their inhabitants. In a society where the individual had no place except as a member of a family, clan, or tribe, and where responsibility in matters such as blood guilt, for example, traditionally reposed in a kinship group rather than an individual, these measures evoked no surprise or resentment.

The Eritrean battalions of the Italian army made an important contribution to the pacification of the country. By offering Eritrean youth an alternative to banditry, the army absorbed and, in this context, sterilized the more adventurous and consequently dangerous element of society. Military service offered the young tribesman or villager the novelty of travel to North Africa, Somalia, and, later, Ethiopia. Italy's colonial campaigns offered adventure without much risk of death or injury and, in the easy-going atmosphere pervading the army's colonial units, not infrequent opportunities of looting. Those who served with distinction could expect titles and, in some·

The Transition to Autonomy, 1951-2

cases, appointments to chieftainships. Many received pensions or gratuities; all were exempt from taxation and the several communal obligations prescribed by custom or the Government.

The disbandment of the Eritrean battalions in 1941 offered the gravest threat to law and order since the Italians had first pacified the country. Eritrea was overrun with ex-soldiers, who were either without work or found civilian life uncongenial and unrewarding. Many had returned home with rifles, ammunition, and hand-grenades, which they hoarded against the future. Arms lay abandoned on the battlefields and concealed in a variety of widely dispersed stores and caches. The balance was tipped dangerously in favour of disorder. The smooth, well-handled transition from the Italian to the British régime, the high level of British prestige after the East African campaign, and the presence in the country of a comparatively large military force delayed but could not prevent an eventual eruption. It first came, as we have seen (pp. 70–71 above), when armed gangs of Bani Amir tribesmen, significantly under the leadership of a former corporal, became engaged in open warfare with the Hadendowa on the Sudan frontier during 1942. Disorder spread to the Gash-Setit, where tribal warfare also broke out between the shy Kunama and their predatory neighbours. And, at the same time, some of the Plateau districts on the Ethiopian frontier were disturbed by hit-and-run raiding carried on by small gangs of Eritrean Shifta from hideouts in Ethiopia.

The disorders, however, offered no apparent threat to British authority. The raiding mostly took place in remote regions on the territory's periphery and had little or no effect on its life or government. In the event, the lesser disturbances on the Ethiopian frontier died out, and the more serious disorders in western Eritrea were brought to an end in 1945 by the negotiation of settlements between the rival factions and the grant of an amnesty to the outlaws.

The comparative ease with which peace was restored diverted attention from the uncomfortable fact that the Administration had been unable to put down outlawry by force. The police were by training and outlook a civil constabulary and had shown little aptitude for the rigours of guerrilla warfare. The Sudan Defence Force brigade garrisoning the territory was equipped and trained to fight on conventional military lines and was too inflexible and ponderous for the acrobatics demanded of it by an elusive and swift-footed foe. Both police and military officers were handicapped by their ignorance of the complexities of the local political background and by insufficient and usually tardy information. They were handicapped also by the absence of any recognized machinery to ensure effective co-operation between the Administration and the army. Though they suffered occasional reverses, the outlaws were neither defeated nor even seriously threatened with defeat. They welcomed the amnesty because for the time being they had grown weary of outlawry; but neither they nor any other Eritreans were deceived into believing the offer to be anything more than an expedient. Consequently there was no safeguard against recidivism or imitative adventures elsewhere.

Nevertheless peace was restored, and the British authorities had an opportunity of appraising the quality and adequacy of their security forces. With the end of the war they had every reason to do so. In the restricted parochial sphere of Eritrea peace was more ominous than war. British withdrawals from India, Pakistan, and Burma foreshadowed recession in the Middle East and were calculated to undermine respect for British authority. Debate and discussion on Eritrea's future, and a growing political consciousness, were exciting passions and provoking internal conflict. The changed economic climate of the Middle East and the world beyond was shrivelling the artificial economy which had been built up in Eritrea during the sheltered years of war. And yet, at a time when there was every indication that the threat to law and order was mounting, the police force was reduced from an establishment of 3,200 to 2,500, the police Frontier Striking Force—the only unit to have been raised and trained to combat Shifta—was disbanded, and the military garrison was reduced from a brigade to a battalion. These measures were largely dictated by a temporary and insolvent Administration's anxiety to economize and the difficulty of obtaining garrison troops once the Sudan Defence Force was no longer on a war establishment. There was, however, little awareness in the Administration of the grave risks which these economies entailed. 'The Shifta have passed into oblivion' was the comfortable comment of the Commissioner of Police.

The Administration was consequently ill prepared for the disturbances which broke out after the departure of the Four Power Commission in January 1948. The security forces were smaller, and, because of the replacement of Sudanese by British troops, even less suited to guerrilla warfare than they had been. The Shifta gangs were more numerous, better armed, and better organized than at the time of the Bani Amir–Hadendowa conflict. By fighting, as it were, under Ethiopian colours they could count on the Christian and predominantly Unionist communities on the Plateau and its fringes for food and shelter, information about the movements of security patrols, and help to deceive the police and soldiery as to

The Transition to Autonomy, 1951–2

their whereabouts. They could count also on covert Ethiopian assistance. It was no secret, for example, that they obtained the bulk of their arms and ammunition from Ethiopia and, when their stocks ran low, could always expect them to be replenished. Moreover the peculiar political complexion of the Shifta disturbances played havoc with the loyalty of the many Christian Abyssinians in the police force, who were mostly Unionist at heart and could not be expected to enter willingly into a struggle against men who, in their eyes, were patriots.

The suddenness with which the disturbances broke out took the Administration by surprise and left it further handicapped by indecision. Opinions as to what should be done were many and conflicting. Many divisional officers were bitterly critical of the quality of the police and pressed for the raising of special irregular units which would operate under their control outside the existing police organization. The police were understandably resentful of this criticism. In their view the answer to the problem was an increase in the police establishment and military garrison. In the event, neither the police force nor the military garrison was increased. An irregular force of Bani Amir tribesmen was, however, raised, only to be disbanded a few weeks later when it took guidance from custom and avenged what the Bani Amir had suffered at the hands of Shifta by inflicting equivalent, though indiscriminate, injury on the Christian Abyssinian communities from which the Shifta had originated.

Many officers also felt that military action alone, whether by troops, police, or irregulars, was unlikely to put an end to the Shifta. They saw little point in limiting the struggle to unrewarding hide-and-seek exercises when there were ways of dealing the Shifta much more telling and easily given blows. Collective punishment of the villages and families from which the Shifta originated and the seizure of bonds from them against the surrender of Shifta were the kind of measures they had in mind. Some also urged that action should be taken against Unionist leaders as a means of inducing Ethiopians and Unionists to withdraw their covert support from the Shifta.

Such views were stoutly resisted by the Administration's Legal Adviser, who was opposed to arbitrary and collective punishment on principle and had argued that if there was evidence of Unionist leaders or others having aided or abetted the Shifta, they should be dealt with by normal judicial processes. Opinions of this kind sounded well in the conference rooms but exasperated divisional officers and police officers who knew that no witness would risk reprisals by giving evidence in court. In the event the Administration steered an uneasy course between the opposing views. A few of the

Eritrea

lesser Unionist leaders were ordered to leave their homes and reside under official surveillance far from the disturbances. Nothing, however, was done in the case of the principal leaders. Collective fines were imposed on a few Abyssinian villages known to have aided Shifta; no action was taken against many other equally or, indeed, more culpable villages, or against the kinsmen of the Shifta. These measures were sufficiently arbitrary to evoke resentment and criticism, but they were too inconsistently and half-heartedly applied to have any lasting effect.

Peace was eventually restored in May 1948. Negotiations between the Christian Abyssinian families from which the Shifta came and the Tigray clans they had attacked were opened to bring about a settlement of the feuds between them. At the same time the Shifta were offered an amnesty. Though they had suffered few reverses they welcomed the amnesty. Many of the rank and file were only part-time adventurers and, with the advent of the summer rains, wanted to go home to cultivate their lands. Nor were the Unionist leaders altogether certain at this time whether their cause was likely to gain more international sympathy than it was losing by their known connexion with the disturbances. Once again peace was purchased without any safeguard against recidivism.

Though the number of Shifta involved had only amounted to about 200, the disorders had taken place in the heart of the territory. Every Eritrean now believed that men could turn Shifta with impunity and that those who fought under Ethiopian colours could count on unusual advantages. The restraints of fifty years of ordered government weakened, allowing the instincts and passions of what was still a backward people to take command of men's minds. The land-hungry Abyssinians on the Plateau, the chiefs who had been deposed during the British and Italian régimes, the aspirants to chieftainships and headmanships, persons (such as the *shumagulle* and landowning *restenya*) who sought to recover privilege and position, the unemployed or ill-paid Abyssinians who were in debt to the Jiberti and resented the prosperity of the Italian industrialist and concessionaire, and indeed the whole conglomerate of aggrieved and ambitious men in the Unionist Party began to contemplate force as the best means of achieving their particular ends.

As we have seen, disorders broke out afresh in 1949 in the form of a Unionist reply to the Independence Bloc. Without doubt they had been politically inspired, but it was wrong to suppose that the Shifta were altruistic young patriots, acting from political motives alone. They were mainly concerned to further their own interests, and the fact that these coincided with those of the Unionist Party

The Transition to Autonomy, 1951–2

enabled them to enjoy, or at least expect, Ethiopian and Unionist favour.

During the latter part of 1949 and the early months of 1950 the disturbances, if marked by greater bitterness and savagery, otherwise resembled those which had broken out after the departure of the Four Power Commission. Italians were attacked in their homes and travelling on the roads; farms and gold mines were raided and ransacked; and on the western flanks of the Plateau, where the settlements negotiated between the Christian Abyssinian villages and the Bani Amir in 1948 had never been enforced, inter-communal conflict broke out once more. But disorder is as capricious as a fire. Sparks fly out fortuitously to expire harmlessly or to set off further conflagrations. In 1948 the fire had subsided without spreading; during 1950 it spread rapidly throughout the most vital areas of Eritrea.

The most combustible material caught fire first. The structure of Eritrean political unity, erected during the Italian régime, had concealed the fundamental conflicts of culture and interest among the Eritrean communities. The Italian régime had had the effect of anaesthetizing the passions dividing them and had lent the lie of Eritrean unity a semblance of truth. With the passing of that régime this anaesthetic effect wore off; and in the sharp climate of wartime and, even more, of post-war Eritrea, sensibility, long numbed but never destroyed, began to return.

In the event bitter, savage, and often unreasoning conflict broke out between Eritrean and Eritrean wherever their interests or cultures clashed. Fighting between the Christian villagers of the Hamasain and Serai and the Moslem Bani Amir assumed a new and ugly ferocity. Fighting broke out once more between the Kunama and their unwelcome neighbours in the old battle-ground of the Gash-Setit Lowlands, and, just as fiercely, between the Moslem Saho and their Christian neighbours in the Akelli Guzai. On the Plateau itself the sturdy Moslem minority in the Serai clashed with the Christian majority and, with help from the Bani Amir and to some extent from the Saho, gave a surprisingly good account of itself. The small, feeble Moslem minority in the Hamasain, after a brief effervescence, was terrorized into inactive silence. On the northern flanks of the Plateau occasional clashes occurred between the villagers of the Hamasain and the Tigray clans of the Coastal Plain. The only parts of Eritrea to which the conflagration did not spread were the territory's remote extremities—the Northern Highlands and the Dankali Lowlands.

Disorder bred further disorder. As the disturbances spread and as

Eritrea

the security forces became farther extended, opportunities of exploiting the situation increased also. A series of bitter attacks against a number of Plateau chiefs were clearly, if not provenly, instigated by their rivals through the instrument of hired Shifta. Most Shifta exploited the situation as best they could. They robbed travellers, looted livestock, blackmailed Italian agriculturists into paying them protection money, and, above all, held up and looted rail and road traffic.

Although no Eritrean, Italian, or British officer had ever doubted that the Unionist Party and Ethiopian Government had instigated the disturbances few seriously credited them with having intended so general a conflagration. Once the United Nations Commission had completed its task the Unionist Party had reason to halt the disturbances which, by emphasizing Eritrean disunity, threatened to damage rather than enhance its interests. Also, however much Ethiopia might have had to gain from provoking disorder in the past, as the sovereign power designate she had nothing to gain from it in the future.

It was, however, too late. Throughout 1950 and the earlier part of 1951 the situation deteriorated progressively. The only noticeable effect of the withdrawal of Ethiopian patronage from the Shifta was that they now, for the first time, began to attack the lesser police posts and smaller patrols to refresh their stocks of ammunition and replace unserviceable rifles. Being denied their principal source of past supply, they could have done nothing else but surrender. In the hope that they might do so the Administration resorted to its tried expedient of offering the Shifta yet a further amnesty in January 1951. Only 296, or barely a tenth of the Shifta then in the field, came in; and within a few months many had broken their word and returned to their old ways. Two months later the Ethiopian Government, by agreement with the Administration, offered asylum and employment to a number of Shifta leaders and their followers. Its offer met with no better result.

This was the position at the time when Sr. Anze Matienzo made his decision to suspend his activities. The situation in the country was serious but, at the same time, the prospect of improvement was better than it had been. After months of unrewarding struggle the security forces were at last achieving results; the comparative measure of their success being reflected in the fact that they inflicted 192 casualties on the Shifta in 1950 as against only 48 during 1948 and 1949. During 1950 the military garrison had been increased by a second British battalion and an additional 500 men had been recruited to the police. Moreover a field force with a strength of about

The Transition to Autonomy, 1951-2

1,800 had been recruited, trained, and equipped solely with the object of combating Shifta. It conformed closely with what many Divisional Officers had been demanding a year before.

There was also a great improvement in the organization of the anti-Shifta campaign. Previously, failure to distinguish between the strategic and tactical spheres and to relate functional responsibilities to them, over-centralization resulting in capricious interference by the central authority with those in the field, and unco-ordinated activity, often vitiated by ignorance of local conditions and poor intelligence, had hampered and enfeebled the Administration. These weaknesses were eliminated, or at least modified, during 1950. A joint civil-military security committee, comprising representatives of the Administration, police, and army, was set up with an overall responsibility, at the strategic level, for planning the anti-Shifta campaign; an officer of the Administration was appointed Staff Officer Anti-Shifta, with the function of co-ordinating the efforts of Administration, police, and army, in accordance with the plans and general policy drawn up by the committee. At the tactical level, in the divisions, plans were drawn up by the Divisional Officers in consultation with the officers in charge of the local police and military detachments. At the same time a useful system of intelligence was established. Information was more systematically obtained, better collated, and more speedily and widely disseminated through intelligence centres at the territorial and divisional levels. The Administration and security forces were consequently able to work in greater harmony and with a better understanding of their task and its multiple implications.

The Administration also derived benefit from the withdrawal of Ethiopian and Unionist favour from the Shifta. Apart from the loss of material aid, the Christian Abyssinian Shifta now began to find their activities hampered by the less friendly, and at times hostile, attitude of a widening circle of the Plateau population. So long as they could boast the style of 'patriots' villagers had been prepared to help them. Once their claim to the title was forfeit they lost their right to sympathy and help. This had a good effect also on the Christian Abyssinian element in the police force, which was now able to serve without shame or fear of reprisals.

Nevertheless the fact remained that the disturbances had increased rather than diminished after the United Nations decision and that there seemed to be no prospect of their abating. As against a monthly average of 85 Shifta incidents during 1950, the figure had risen to 130 in May 1951 at the time when Sr. Anze Matienzo had made his announcement. The feeling that the only practicable way of restor-

Eritrea

ing order speedily was to offer the Shifta a general amnesty gained ground. The argument naturally found favour in Ethiopian and Unionist circles, where a genuine desire for ending the Shifta nuisance was in conflict with a sense of obligation towards those who had served Ethiopia's cause. It found favour with the Italians, who were now desperately anxious for peace at any price. It also gained the support of the United Nations High Commissioner.

The Administration's experience of amnesties in the past had not been happy. Without adequate safeguards against recidivism, a fresh amnesty might earn no better dividends than the past ones. There was also the difficulty that a general amnesty embracing all Shifta would put the Administration in the position of pardoning criminals guilty, in some cases, of the most savage barbarities. Nevertheless the problem had to be solved speedily if the United Nations decision was to be implemented. Only a general and unconditional amnesty seemed likely to bring about a speedy solution. One was accordingly proclaimed on 19 June 1951; and by the end of August it was estimated that at least 90 per cent. of the Shifta had surrendered.

To consolidate what had been achieved, active measures had to be taken to round up, or at least neutralize, the remaining Shifta and prevent recidivism. A new security proclamation was published for the purpose. The Chief Administrator was empowered to set up special courts with an accelerated procedure to enable Shifta cases to be disposed of expeditiously; he was also empowered to confirm death sentences, which had previously had to be referred to London. At the same time the Chief Administrator acquired powers to levy collective fines and take bonds from communities where there was good reason to believe that Shifta had been directly or indirectly aided. Armed with these powers the Administration was in a better position than it had ever been to restore law and order. Even so, much depended on how it acted.

It acted promptly and vigorously. The security forces, which were now relieved of many of their previous commitments, were redeployed against the few gangs who were still active. In each district the village and tribal communities were made responsible for security within their own boundaries, and liable to punishment for failure to discharge their responsibilities adequately. Stern measures had to be taken against a few communities to demonstrate the Administration's determination. They did not go unrewarded. For example when an Italian farmer was abducted by a band of Shifta the Administration secured his release on the same day by seizing ten men and a hundred head of cattle against his return from the village near to the scene of the outrage. Action such as this had a speedy

The Transition to Autonomy, 1951-2

and widespread effect. From assisting Shifta, or at least conniving at their activities, villagers began to co-operate openly with the Administration, aiding the security forces with information and, on several occasions, attacking and even capturing Shifta.

It was realized, however, that unless the many, bitter feuds were settled, security would remain in continual jeopardy. Accordingly conciliation courts were set up to examine the claims and counter-claims of rival communities, determine compensation for the injuries they had sustained, and provide for their peaceful behaviour in future. At first there was some reluctance to submit to arbitration or to respect the authority of the courts. In each case firm action was taken to put an end to intransigence. Eventually the various disputes were brought before the courts; judgements were given and executed; and peace was restored.

By July 1951 security had sufficiently improved to allow the Administration and United Nations Commissioner to return to the task of putting the United Nations decision into effect. Had the Administration not shown itself resolute many more months might have passed before order was restored. Fortunately, at this critical time, it had a Chief Administrator of unusual determination. Mr. (now Sir Duncan) Cumming[2] had brought with him a wealth of experience from previous service in the Sudan and as the Chief Civil Affairs Officer responsible for all the former Italian Colonies. His leadership and commanding personality revived the weary and dispirited officers serving in the divisions and gained the immediate respect of tribal and village leaders. He was primarily responsible for introducing and enforcing the system of communal responsibility which finally ended the disorders. Whether this would have had the same results at the time when the Shifta enjoyed Ethiopian and Unionist sympathy must remain a matter for conjecture. The pity was that it was never put to the test.

THE CONSTITUTIONAL PROBLEM

The General Assembly of the United Nations had decided that Eritrea was to be 'an autonomous unit federated with Ethiopia under the sovereignty of the Ethiopian Crown'. She was to have full 'legislative, executive, and judicial powers in the field of domestic affairs'; the Federal Government was to have jurisdiction in defence, foreign affairs, finance and currency, foreign and inter-state communications. An 'Imperial Federal Council' was to be set up to

---

[2] Mr D. C. Cumming succeeded Brigadier F. G. Drew as Chief Administrator in 1951. The latter had been Chief Administrator since 1946, when he succeeded Brigadier J. M. Benoy, CBE.

Eritrea

advise on federal affairs. Eritreans were to be represented in the federal Legislature 'in accordance with law', and 'in the proportion that the population of Eritrea bears to the population of the Federation'. Similarly, Eritreans were to be represented in the executive and judicial branches of the Federal Government.[3] The terms of the resolution were commendably brief and simple, but, in being so, left much that should have been said unsaid. Deliberate ambiguities and, indeed, evasions of contentious issues did little to illuminate the difficult path which Sr. Anze Matienzo, the United Nations Commissioner, was now required to tread.

There were several incongruities about the Federation envisaged by the resolution. As one of the two units comprising it was very much larger than the other and already a sovereign state, it was difficult to visualize how any reasonable balance could be achieved, more especially as Sr. Anze Matienzo was required to provide Eritrea with a constitution 'based on the principles of democratic government',[4] which would contrast oddly with the authoritarianism of the Ethiopian monarchy. Moreover, a constitution was to be drafted for Eritrea, but none for the Federal Government; nor was it clear whether a separate Federal Government was intended at all, or whether the Ethiopian Government was expected to combine the functions of a federal and a State authority. Problems such as these, and the difficulty of converting a deeply divided and backward people, who knew nothing about federation, to faith in it, and of reconciling their views with those of Ethiopia now confronted Sr. Anze Matienzo.

Nevertheless Sr. Anze Matienzo set about his task with admirable optimism. He addressed innumerable press conferences and gatherings of Eritreans. Federation he described as 'a middle of the road plan which should give satisfaction not only to those who want to be united with Ethiopia, but to those who want Eritrea to be independent.'[5] He made an undoubted impression on his Eritrean and Italian audiences and evoked what he had every reason to believe was a highly satisfactory response. All the political parties pledged themselves 'to respect . . . the decision to federate Eritrea with Ethiopia in conformity with the principles . . . approved by the General Assembly . . .' and 'to give the best possible cooperation to the Commissioner of the United Nations with a view to drafting the constitution. . . .'[6] As a gesture of its acceptance of federation the Independence Bloc changed its title to the Democratic Bloc. And on the anniversary of the deplorable riots which had greeted the United

---

[3] *Final Report of U.N. Commissioner* (A/2188), pp. 74–75.   [4] Ibid. p. 75.
[5] A/1959, p. 16.   [6] Ibid. p. 71.

The Transition to Autonomy, 1951-2

Nations Commission the previous year, Moslem and Christian representatives went together to place flowers on the victims' graves.

Once the Shifta problem had been disposed of, Sr. Anze Matienzo addressed himself to the task of consulting the inhabitants about the draft constitution. Preliminary discussions had revealed fairly wide differences of opinion between himself on the one hand and the Ethiopian Government and British Administration on the other. Ato Aklilu, the Ethiopian Foreign Minister, argued that, since the draft had to be submitted to a representative assembly of Eritreans, there was no purpose in any consultation. The Administration, which was anxious to avoid arousing unnecessary excitement, proposed that Sr. Anze Matienzo should consult the representatives of the political parties either separately or collectively as an advisory council. Sr. Anze Matienzo, however, insisted that his task was to consult the inhabitants; and to this end he announced that he proposed to do so on the lines adopted by the two visiting Commissions. Like them he arranged to receive deputations from political parties and social, cultural, professional, and commercial associations in Asmara, and then tour the territory to meet gatherings of 'representatives' at each centre.

Sr. Anze Matienzo's perambulations had just the effect which both the Ethiopian Government and British Administration had hoped to avoid. The publicity attending his activities, and the efforts of the political leaders to parade the largest possible gatherings of supporters at each centre he visited, quickly rekindled the passions which had begun to die down and soured the atmosphere of comparative goodwill which had so recently come into being. The local press swiftly reverted to irresponsible abuse, and Ibrahim Sultan, now the Secretary General of the Democratic Bloc, published such inflammatory matter that the Administration found it necessary to caution him. At the same time an ugly incident in which Ato Woldeab Woldemariam[7] survived a hand-grenade attack—the sixth attempt on his life—threatened a fresh outbreak of terrorism. The Chief Administrator prudently lost no time in summoning the political leaders and warning them that he would take action against them if they continued to threaten the peace.

Nor could Sr. Anze Matienzo congratulate himself on the outcome of his travels. His investigations revealed much sharper differences of opinion than he had foreseen. 'The political parties appear to be determined to maintain their former differences of view, [he wrote] and have not shown the expected spirit of conciliation....'[8]

[7] See above, p. 65.   [8] A/1959, p. 74.

Eritrea

Behind all the voluble lip-service to the principle of federation, the Ethiopian Government and the Eritrean parties clearly remained wedded to their former views. The Ethiopians were intent on a federation which would in practice leave full control in the Emperor's hands; the Unionists were of a similar, if not the same, view, but the Democratic Bloc and the Moslem League of the Western Province, though still divided, were anxious that the unwelcome link with Ethiopia should be no more than a tenuous formality. Only the small and inactive Liberal Unionist Party had any sincere desire for federation.

Whatever form the constitution took, the key to control in a country such as Eritrea would lie in the Executive. And so, when Sr. Anze Matienzo began his consultations with Ato Aklilu, he soon found that Ethiopia was determined to gain control over the Eritrean Executive. Ato Aklilu surveyed most of the existing federations and pointed out that, in each, the Federal Government had a much greater measure of control over the federated units than was envisaged by the United Nations resolution in the case of the Eritrean-Ethiopian federation. In Eritrea the Federal Government, though responsible for the integrity of the Federation, would have no means of exercising its jurisdiction, for example in the matter of collecting federal revenue, except through the Eritrean Government. Accordingly he demanded that the balance should be redressed by empowering the Emperor to appoint all executive officials in Eritrea, including a Governor General, and to approve or reject all legislation. In brief, what the Ethiopian Government sought was an arrangement which would ensure the appointment of a reliable Unionist to every key position in the Eritrean Government.

Ato Aklilu also showed a good deal of concern over proposals raised by leaders of the Democratic Bloc that Eritrea should have its own flag and that its official languages should be Tigrinya and Arabic. He claimed that Eritrea was not a separate state and therefore had no right to a separate flag, which would be contrary to the 'close political and economic association' between Eritrea and Ethiopia demanded by the United Nations resolution.[9] Similarly it was unacceptable that Amharic, the official language of the Empire, should be excluded from Eritrea. He did not object to the use of Tigrinya and Arabic by Eritreans in official matters, but he insisted that, as elsewhere in the Federation, Amharic should be the sole official language of Eritrea.

Sr. Anze Matienzo did not find Ato Aklilu's views endorsed during his tour around the territory. The Democratic Bloc and the Moslem

[9] *Final Report of U.N. Commissioner* (A/2188), p. 74.

The Transition to Autonomy, 1951–2

League of the Western Province were completely opposed to the Ethiopian Government being represented in Eritrea, demanding that the head of the Executive should be an Eritrean and should be elected locally. The majority of the Unionists were agreeable to the Emperor being represented in Eritrea by a Governor General, provided that the latter's powers were limited to approving the appointment of an elected head of the Eritrean Executive. In the matter of the official languages, the Unionists were even less amenable to Ethiopian views, countering the proposals sponsored by the Democratic Bloc and the Moslem League of the Western Province with the somewhat perverse demand that Tigrinya alone should be Eritrea's official language. It was only in the matter of the flag that they were prepared to toe the Ethiopian line, opposing the Democratic Bloc and the Moslem League of the Western Province, who insisted that Eritrea and the Federation should both have their own flags, since in their view the Ethiopian flag was a State and not a federal symbol.

There were less serious differences over what form Eritrea's Legislature should take. The Democratic Bloc proposed that it should comprise a Senate and an elected Assembly: a device designed to provide adequate checks in the upper house should the Unionists gain control of the lower. For similar reasons the Ethiopian Government and the Unionists favoured a single elected Assembly. The Moslem League of the Western Province suggested two regional Assemblies, one for the Moslem and one for the Christian Abyssinian districts. By this ingenious plan they sought to partition Eritrea as they had previously desired and to federate each of its halves with Ethiopia.

Sr. Anze Matienzo left Eritrea in November 1951 to consider the problems arising out of his consultations and to take advice from three lawyers of distinction: Sir Ivor Jennings, the British constitutionalist, Dr. Rijpperda Wierdsma, the Dutch jurist, and Dr. Paul Guggenheim of Geneva University, where he later became Professor of Public International Law. Before leaving, he gave Ato Aklilu some idea of his reactions to the proposals and counter-proposals before him. He agreed that the Ethiopian Government should also be the Federal Government and that the Emperor should be represented in Eritrea by a Governor General. But since Eritrea was to be an 'autonomous unit' and have 'the widest possible measure of self-government', he felt that the Emperor's representative should not control the Eritrean Executive. He saw no reason why Eritrea should not have a flag of its own, since many Federated States in America and elsewhere had their individual flags. And as for the

Eritrea

language question he considered that this was essentially a matter in which Eritrean wishes should prevail.

While Sr. Anze Matienzo was engaged in the study of these constitutional issues, the Administration had to set about arranging for and convoking a representative assembly of the Eritrean people to consider the constitution which was being drafted by the United Nations Commissioner. It had, of course, already broken the ground by arranging the election of representatives to appear before the Four Power Commission. Even so there was a wide difference between the rough-and-ready 'elections' of 1947 and those envisaged by the General Assembly's resolution. An electoral system and procedure had not only to be planned but, before they could be implemented, to be understood and accepted by the Eritreans.

The first problem was to decide what method of election should be used. Direct elections by secret ballot were only practicable in the towns. Among the widely dispersed and mainly nomadic tribes they were out of the question; and though it would have been possible to hold them in the settled village communities on the Plateau, the time-table was far too narrow to leave room for the laborious and possibly contentious task of registration.

In the event the Administration decided to adopt the same electoral arrangements as had been introduced in the Sudan to meet a similar problem. Direct elections by secret ballot would be held in the two major towns of Asmara and Massawa, but elsewhere village and family groups would elect representatives in customary fashion to regional electoral colleges, which would in their turn elect regional representatives by secret ballot.

A subsidiary problem was that of deciding what the constituencies were to be. It was essential that these should be of approximately the same size in terms of population, and desirable (if they were to be locally acceptable) that each should comprise a reasonably homogeneous social group. So neatly divided was the population in its political views that the slightest degree of over-representation in any area would be likely to have serious consequences. It needed considerable ingenuity to devise constituencies which would satisfy both criteria. A way was nevertheless found. Sixty-eight constituencies were established, each with an approximate population of 15,000 and conforming generally with a recognizable social or tribal group. The only serious criticism came from the Unionists, who complained that the population figures on which the Administration had worked were inaccurate and favoured the Moslem communities. The complaint was a resentful echo of representations they had made to both the Four Power and United Nations Commissions.

The Transition to Autonomy, 1951-2

A further issue was that of whether the half-caste 'Italo-Eritreans' were entitled to electoral rights. The Ethiopian Government and the Unionists were naturally concerned lest they should be given an opportunity to join forces with the Eritrean supporters of the Democratic Bloc. The decision in the matter was left to the Administration. Though the General Assembly's resolution made no specific provision for this particular contingency, it had ruled that

> All inhabitants born in Eritrea and having at least one indigenous parent or grandparent shall also be nationals of the Federation. Such persons, if in possession of a foreign nationality, shall, within six months of the coming into force of the Eritrean Constitution, be free to opt to renounce the nationality of the Federation and retain such foreign nationality.[10]

In the light of this, Sr. Anze Matienzo was of the opinion that half-castes eligible for federal citizenship should also have electoral rights, since they were potential federal citizens. Ato Aklilu argued that, until the federation came into being, no half-caste could in fact be a federal citizen and, accordingly, that none should enjoy electoral rights. In the event the Administration compromised between the two view-points, deciding that only those half-castes who were not foreign nationals should have the right to vote.

The various issues were determined, and the approved electoral arrangements set forth, in a proclamation published on 29 January 1952. The elections were to take place during March; the 'primary' elections to the electoral colleges in the rural areas at the beginning of the month, and the final (and in the towns direct) elections at the end. Before this, during February, electors in Asmara and Massawa were required to register. In the constituencies responsibility for the supervision and arrangement of the elections was given to committees composed of representatives of the principal political parties under British chairmanship.

The elections took place without the least disturbance; and, indeed, with somewhat less interest and excitement than some of the political leaders found flattering. In the rural areas polling was high, almost 100 per cent. of the members of the electoral colleges voting. In the urban constituencies, surprisingly, only about 88 per cent. of the registered voters went to the polls; and they represented only that half of the potential electorate who had cared to register. Now that there was less Italian and Ethiopian money in circulation, political conflict and passions were less easily aroused.

The election results revealed in unequivocal fashion how the country divided politically and what the strength of the various

[10] *Final Report of U.N. Commissioner* (A/2188), p. 74.

Eritrea

parties was. The 68 seats were neatly divided between Christian and Moslem candidates. The Unionists won 32, the Democratic Bloc 18, and the Moslem League of the Western Province 15. The 3 remaining seats were divided between the Independent Moslem League, the Nationalist Party, and an independent candidate. The Unionists captured the great majority of Plateau constituencies but had few successes elsewhere. The Moslem League of the Western Province was successful in most Western Province constituencies; and one of its candidates even succeeded in forcing a tie in the primary election where Ibrahim Sultan was standing as the Democratic Bloc representative. The Bloc won a few seats in the Western Province, but its strength came mainly from the coastal and Saho tribes and the Moslem populations of Asmara and Massawa.

As a result of the elections the Moslem League of the Western Province found itself holding the balance between the Unionists and the Bloc. Although its leaders shared many of the Bloc's views, there was so much bitterness and rivalry between them and Ibrahim Sultan that an alliance could not easily have been brought about. If the Unionist leaders had adopted the extreme Ethiopian line they and the Bloc would certainly have come together. As it was the Unionist Party was at this time subject to the pressure of a growing body of its supporters who, though pro-Ethiopian, were determined that Eritrea's interests should not be subordinated to Ethiopia's.

Accordingly the Unionist leaders had no difficulty in adopting a sufficiently moderate tone to win the support of the League. By turning their backs on their old allies in the Democratic Bloc and joining forces with what had been their common enemy, the League had tipped the balance in the Unionists' favour. Ibrahim Sultan and his colleagues in the Democratic Bloc sourly accused their leaders of having sold their Moslem followers for appointments in the future Government of Eritrea. Kinder observers commented that, having at last faced the fact that federation was unavoidable, they had decided to make the best of it.

Sr. Anze Matienzo's draft constitution would never have been accepted if either the Unionists or Democratic Bloc had enjoyed an overall majority. Its terms did, however, closely conform with the compromise view on which the Unionists and the Moslem League of the Western Province had agreed, and, as a result, it was approved with only minor modifications.[11] It provided for a Governor General appointed by the Emperor with the simple functions of promulgating Eritrean legislation and reading the speech from the throne. He was also to have the power of referring back for reconsideration by the

[11] The text was published in *Final Report of U.N. Commissioner* (A/2188), pp. 76–89.

The Transition to Autonomy, 1951–2

Legislature any legislation which, in his opinion, encroached on the jurisdiction of the Federal Government or involved 'international responsibility'. The Legislature was to be a single Assembly and was to have an elected President. The Executive was to be in charge of a 'Chief Executive' who would be elected by the Assembly and would appoint 'Secretaries' to take charge of the departments of government. He was also to appoint judges, on the recommendation of the President of the Assembly, but not other officials, who were to be appointed by a Civil Service Commission.

Thus, the draft carefully insulated the Eritrean Government against undue Ethiopian control and, in recognition of Eritrea's autonomous status, permitted it to have its own flag and, as its official languages, Tigrinya and Arabic. Though the Ethiopian Government could scarcely have welcomed so direct a rejection of its views on every point on which it had taken issue, the Unionist representatives in the Assembly approved the constitution without demur.

The Transfer of Power

While the Eritrean constitution was being drafted the British Administration had to prepare to lay down its authority on or before 15 September 1952. It had to transfer responsibility to both the Federal Ethiopian and the Eritrean Governments. It had to set up an Eritrean Government and ensure that its structure conformed with a constitution which was in the making but not made. Also it had to 'induct Eritreans into all levels'[12] of an Administration which was still largely in the hands of aliens. In short, at the same time as it was abdicating its own authority, it had to conduct a major revolution in the shortest possible time and with the least disturbance to the life of the country.

The transfer of power to the Federal Ethiopian Government offered no serious difficulty. The major problem was to transfer power to an Eritrean Government which had still to be set up. The British Administration, so long as it remained responsible for governing Eritrea, had to be free to act as it thought fit during what might be a period of crisis. The risk entailed in transferring power progressively to unpractised and possibly irresponsible hands at such a time was too great. But, since an Eritrean Legislature had to be in being when the new Government assumed control, and therefore, presumably, had to be set up during the lifetime of the British Administration, it was difficult to see how this could be avoided. This particular problem and the whole business of arranging for the election

[12] *Final Report of U.N. Commissioner* (A/2188), p. 75.

Eritrea

of a Legislature were happily disposed of by a convenient decision that the Representative Assembly, though intended only as a form of constituent body, should become the Eritrean Legislature as soon as the Emperor ratified the constitution.[13]

The setting up of an Eritrean Judiciary was a more complicated affair. As we have seen, the British Administration had managed to adapt the Italian system to its own short-term purposes; but the difference between the system which had evolved and what was demanded by the constitution was too great to be satisfied by any further patching. The constitution provided for a Supreme Court and subordinate courts which were all to be free of the Legislature and Executive.[14] Since the existing Judiciary was under the control of the Executive and there was no Supreme Court, what the constitution implied was a new judicial system rather than a modification of the one in being. To make the change during what remained of the British Administration's life would have been difficult and in many respects inconvenient. It was finally agreed that a special committee composed of British legal officers, Italian judges, and the United Nations Commissioner and his legal consultants should devise an appropriate system and draft suitable legislation, so as to enable it to be established on the transfer of power.

The Judiciary proposed by this committee was to consist of a Supreme Court, a High Court of Justice, and District Courts. All judges of the Supreme Court and not less than half of the judges of the High Court were to be legal practitioners, or the holders of law degrees for at least seven years. The Supreme Court was to be a court of final appeal, the judge of questions involving the jurisdiction of other courts, and the sole authority for interpreting the constitution. The High Court was to be a court of criminal issues and an appeal court in the first instance from the District Courts. With the exception of the cases reserved to the High Court, the District Courts were to enjoy unlimited jurisdiction in all civil and criminal issues. The chiefs and sub-chiefs, being executive authorities, were to be deprived of their judicial powers, but, in recognition of custom and the practical convenience of litigants, they were to be free to act as arbiters in civil issues at the request of the parties in dispute, and their decisions were to be registered in the District Courts.

Three types of law were to be administered. First, there was statutory law, which would include such British and Italian statutory law as the new Eritrean Government approved, the laws it subsequently enacted, and, for a time at least, the Italian Penal Code; secondly,

---

[13] Art. 99 of constitution (*Final Report of U.N. Commissioner* (A/2188), p. 89).
[14] Arts. 85 and 86 (*Final Report of U.N. Commissioner* (A/2188), pp. 87–88).

The Transition to Autonomy, 1951-2

Moslem *Sharia* Law; and finally, local customary law in all its multiple varieties. In each type of court different judges were to be appointed to administer each category of law and in each court there were to be separate criminal and civil divisions. In criminal cases statutory law would be applied. In civil cases the type of law would be determined by the parties. Special rules were drawn up to provide against their disagreement.

In planning the transfer of power it soon became apparent that if there was to be any reasonable continuity of government, some formal body empowered to act on behalf of the future Eritrean Government would have to be set up. Firm and durable decisions were needed on a variety of matters. A budget had to be prepared; the conditions of service of the new Government's employees had to be drawn up, and contracts had to be made with them; agreements had to be concluded for the provision of supplies; new appointments had to be made; old legislation had to be revised and new legislation prepared; and decisions had to be taken on many other matters of substance. For this purpose an Eritrean Executive Committee was elected by the Eritrean Representative Assembly and, by the inclusion of a special clause in the Eritrean constitution, it received retrospective authority to act on behalf of the future Eritrean Government.

In setting up an Eritrean Executive the British Administration had to devise some arrangement whereby it could transfer power simultaneously to the Federal Ethiopian and Eritrean Governments. Its first step was to reorganize itself into two branches: one dealing with federal subjects and the other with those which would fall within the sphere of the Eritrean Government. It was felt that this arrangement would ensure a smooth transfer of power, and would also enable the second of the two branches, which took the title of Eritrean Affairs Secretariat, to develop as the Executive of the Eritrean Government.

The constitution envisaged an Executive under the control of a Chief Executive assisted by Secretaries of Executive Departments who would be appointed by the Chief Executive and would enjoy a quasi-ministerial status. The Administration was naturally disinclined to introduce a ministerial system before the transfer of power; and therefore it was decided to set up the executive departments of the future Government, but to place them under the control of the Chief Administrator. The Chief Executive and Secretaries would be appointed but would not assume office until power had been transferred.

It was envisaged that the future Eritrean Executive would be

Eritrea

organized as four departments. First, the Department of the Interior, with responsibility for district administration, police, prisons, municipalities, public works, and the government press; second, the Financial Department (finance and accounts, excise, commerce, and establishments); third, the Department of Economic Affairs (agriculture, forestry, veterinary affairs, industry, internal trade, communications, mines, minerals, and state lands); and, fourth, the Department of Social Affairs (education, health, and labour). The permanent official at the head of the Executive would be a Director General responsible to the Chief Executive; each department would be under the immediate control of a Deputy Director answerable politically to the appropriate Secretary and, administratively, to the Director General. The Departments for the Interior and Social Affairs were set up, but not those for Financial and Economic Affairs, since it was impracticable to separate the federal and Eritrean aspects of finance and economics. These two departments of the new Eritrean Affairs Secretariat were placed in charge of British officers, assisted by Eritreans who would take over after the transfer of power.

A more exacting task was that of 'inducting Eritreans into all levels of the Administration'. During the first phase of the Occupation much had been done to replace Italians by Eritreans in the lower levels of the Administration, but, subsequently, the process of Eritreanization had almost come to a standstill. In departments such as Public Works, Agriculture, Veterinary Affairs, Forestry, and Health it was notorious that the Administration's efforts to Eritreanize had been thwarted by the Italian technical officers in charge. They had been trained to seek technical efficiency and knew that they could achieve the best results with trained Italian subordinates. When political considerations demand a policy which, in a technical context, is questionable, technical officers can seldom be left freedom to carry it out.

In the event the issue could no longer be evaded. The Administration, therefore, announced, that except where efficiency might be reduced to 'a dangerously low level', posts would be Eritreanized. Notices were published inviting applications for employment, and at the same time courses of instruction were arranged for a wide variety of posts ranging from typists to electricians and from plumbers to wireless operators. The candidates were first required to pass the simplest of tests in reading and writing in English, Italian, Arabic, or Tigrinya. Those who passed took a course of training, at the end of which they had to pass a simple qualifying examination before being accepted into the Administration. The quality of the

The Transition to Autonomy, 1951-2

Eritrean candidates was even lower than had been expected. Of 1,140 candidates who passed the first test and subsequently took a clerical training course, only 189 were able to qualify for permanent employment. Nevertheless Eritreans took over more than 1,000 posts from Italians, and the proportion left in Italian hands was negligible.

The Eritreanization of the police force was undertaken without difficulty. Eritreans took readily to police work and there were a number of efficient and knowledgeable Eritrean inspectors available for promotion. Arrangements were made for some of these inspectors to receive training in the United Kingdom; and special courses for n.c.o.'s and inspectors were organized in Eritrea. Gradually all but the central direction and administration of the force passed into Eritrean hands. More than 1,000 Eritreans were 'inducted' into the force.

The Eritreanization of administrative appointments was more difficult. The senior departmental appointments in the Secretariat were filled by the more experienced Eritrean Administrative Assistants, the best of whom became understudies to the British officers in charge of the departments and sections. The appointments in the divisions and districts were less easy to fill. Though there were Eritrean Administrative Assistants available, they were mostly young men who had had to rely on strong British backing to exercise their authority. Because of this it was decided that well-known men of local standing and influence from outside the Administration should be appointed Governors of what had been known as divisions but would become provinces. Each would be assisted by an Executive Secretary appointed from among the senior Eritrean Administrative Assistants. Where possible the officers in charge of the districts into which the provinces would be subdivided would be appointed from the Eritrean Administrative Assistants. Gradually British officers were replaced by Eritreans in the divisions and districts, until only those in charge of divisions and seated in the chairs of the future Governors were left. The Executive Committee refused to designate any Eritreans for these posts, on the ground that their appointment concerned the Civil Service Commission provided for under the constitution.

At the time of the transfer of power only 348 foreigners remained in the employment of the Administration, as against 2,217 who had been serving it a year earlier. About 260 of those who remained were engaged in subordinate posts as technicians; the rest held senior appointments. The question of engaging foreigners had occupied a good deal of the Executive Committee's attention: its anxiety to retain the services of foreigners in certain posts being as great as its concern to expel them from others. In addition to technical officers such as doctors and engineers, the Eritrean Government would need help in administrative, financial, and judicial matters. Whether this would be better given in executive or advisory form was examined with some care. The Committee decided to retain British officers in the posts of Financial Adviser and District Advisers. They were also to be engaged as Chief Auditor and as judges. The majority of foreigners left in subordinate posts were Italian; of the senior appointments 55 were held by Italians and 20 by British subjects.

The most important aspect of the precautions for the transfer of power was perhaps the budget. The Ethiopian Government had made it known that it was ready to subsidize the Eritrean Government, implying, however, that, should this become necessary, it would claim a right of control over Eritrea's finances. To preserve its autonomy Eritrea would therefore have to balance its budget. The prospect was gloomy. Because of increased expenditure on security forces the financial year 1950–1 had ended with a deficit of £376,000. The 1951–2 estimates showed an expected deficit of £800,000. Nevertheless a fairly satisfactory budget was drawn up. Revenue was estimated at £1,639,005 and expenditure at £1,566,644; showing a small surplus of £72,361. Almost all revenue was derived from customs, excise, and direct taxes.

Expenditure was considerably reduced as a consequence of the replacement of foreign officials by Eritreans, the reduction of establishments, the simplification of the system of government, the transfer of certain costly services such as the railway, trunk roads, and ports to the federal budget, and a welcome agreement with the Italian Government, whereby the latter undertook to finance educational and health services for the Italian community.[15]

Before power could be transferred certain Organic Laws had to be enacted to enable the constitution to be put into effect, and existing legislation had to be revised to equip the new Government with an initial body of statutory law. The Administration drafted a set of Organic Laws[16] and submitted them to the Executive Committee, but owing to pressure of business this was only able to approve one draft—the Functions of Government Act—before the transfer of power. It was understood that the remainder would be enacted soon afterwards. At the same time the Administration set up a committee to revise existing legislation. Its recommendations were incorporated

[15] See also Resolution 530 (VI) on economic and financial provisions relating to Eritrea, adopted by the General Assembly on 29 January 1952 (*GAOR*, 5th sess., Supplement no. 20 (A/2119), pp. 24–27).
[16] *Final Report of U.N. Commissioner* (A/2188), pp. 59–65.

The Transition to Autonomy, 1951–2

in a draft Revision, Amendment and Interpretation of Laws Proclamation which became law on 11 September.

While these preparations were in train, arrangements were also made for the transfer of power to the Ethiopian or future Federal Government. The United Nations resolution implied that the departments or sections discharging those responsibilities of the Administration which were potentially federal would be transferred to the Federal Government. The position as regards defence, immigration, currency, exchange control, customs, import and export trade, aviation, meteorological services, ports and lighthouses, and posts and telecommunications was quite clear. There was, however, some doubt as to whether the railway, ropeway, and roads were to be a federal responsibility or not. Eritrea's financial interest demanded that they should be, and in support there was the argument that they were not properly 'inter-state' communications. The railway and ropeway, for example, could be considered to be appendages of the port of Massawa, which was a federal responsibility, and it was arguable that, since the main trunk roads linked Eritrea with Ethiopia and the Sudan, they were external communications and consequently also a federal responsibility. This argument was eventually accepted and it was agreed that the Ethiopian Government would accept responsibility for them.

The only serious difficulty encountered was over the question of property. The Federal Government naturally needed the offices, workshops, transport, and all the varieties of buildings and equipment at the disposal of the Eritrean departments it was about to take over. It needed houses for its officials and a suitable residence for the Governor General. In the British view the Administration had power to set aside immovable property for the use of the Federal Government and its officials, but no legal right to transfer ownership. The question of ownership, it held, was one which would have to be settled between the two successor authorities after the transfer of power. There was no dispute as to the disposal of the greater part of the property. There was, however, a good deal of bitter controversy when it came to allocating houses for federal officials. Though the demands of the Ethiopian authorities were not fully met, there was much Eritrean indignation at what was set aside for their use.

When the Emperor of Ethiopia formally ratified the Federal Act[17] on 11 September 1952, the long and complicated processes demanded by the United Nations resolution were sufficiently advanced. The transfer was completed without incident. The Governor General

[17] *Final Report of U.N. Commissioner* (A/2188), pp. 44–47.

Eritrea

designate, the few federal officials appointed to function in Eritrea, and a garrison of Ethiopian troops moved in. The principal officers of the new Eritrean Government took up their appointments. The withdrawal of the last British officials and troops took place. On the evening of 15 September a great multitude witnessed the lowering of the Union Jack in the centre of Asmara and the hoisting of the Ethiopian or, as they now were, federal colours. The United Nations decision had been put into effect. The British Occupation had ended.

Though barely a handful of the British officers left in Eritrea at the transfer of power had been in the country half a dozen years, most had cultivated a real interest in and affection for its people; had this not been so, few would have remained to serve a moribund Administration without financial inducement or promise of future employment. It could not be claimed that they had abandoned the work and interest of a lifetime like the British officials who had left India and Pakistan shortly before; but, as against this, they had not their satisfaction of having remained to complete a mission to which they had been consciously dedicated.

The British had not, of course, had any real mission in Eritrea, being required only to act as caretakers. It was to their credit that they had not interpreted their duties too narrowly, and that they had done what they could to equip Eritreans to handle their own affairs. Set against the impressive progress in many dependent territories since the war, their achievements may seem to have been trivial. But what they had done was not to be measured only in statistics of new schools, dispensaries, hospital beds, and Advisory Councils, and the promotion of Eritreans to posts of responsibility. Their real contribution to Eritrea was that, at some risk and cost to themselves and without any hope of advantage, they had converted a subservient population accustomed to hear and obey the orders of an alien colonial government into a people who were learning to think and act for themselves. Under the wise guidance of Brigadier Longrigg there had been ordered and comparatively rapid progress during the first phase of the Occupation. Subsequently there had been little progress. Not because there had been any change of heart in the Administration; but because Eritrea had been turned into a battlefield by Ethiopian and, later, Italian subversion.

ETHIOPIA AND ERITREA

Eritrea is now an 'autonomous State federated with Ethiopia'. The old colonial régime, which in its Italian and British forms had lasted for more than sixty years, has ended; and authority is now shared by Ethiopians and Eritreans. The transfer of power marked

The Transition to Autonomy, 1951–2

the end of a process of rapid and radical revolution and the beginning of a bold, if perhaps capriciously conceived, experiment. Will it prove successful? Will Eritrea and Ethiopia find contentment in their partnership?

No federal or other constitutional device can paper over Eritrea's fundamental weaknesses: its natural poverty and the disunity of its people. Eritrea's future, and indeed the Federation's, is likely to depend on the extent to which these weaknesses can be overcome. Italian benevolence succeeded in cushioning Eritreans against their poverty, and thereby eased the traditional friction between Moslem and Christian. It was only during the British Occupation, when Eritrea was thrown on to its own resources, that the cracks in the social fabric began to appear. At first, because of the fortuitous circumstances of war, they seemed comparatively trivial; subsequently, after the end of the war, they widened alarmingly, when, under the spur of unemployment and bad wages in the towns and land hunger in the rural districts of the Plateau, the Christian Abyssinians came into bitter and savage conflict with their Moslem neighbours. That, in similar circumstances, they may well do so again is beyond doubt. Easement of economic distress is a pailiative which, as during the Italian régime, may be expected to damp down the fires of communal rivalries but is unlikely to be a durable solution. What is needed, if the threat of serious internal conflict is to be removed, is economic development, the education of sufficient Christians and Moslems to bridge the gap dividing one half of the people from the other, and adequate force to maintain security.

Eritrea has not the means of financing development or even of palliating economic distress. Left to its own resources it would be unable to maintain the comparatively simple educational system existing at the end of the Occupation.[18] Its own revenue could never support sufficient force to maintain security without military backing. It has no alternative but to lean heavily on Ethiopia. Whether it seeks for Ethiopian or foreign financial aid it can only turn to the Ethiopian Government. For military support its own Government must depend on Ethiopian co-operation and goodwill.

It must be remembered that Ethiopia has always contended that Eritrean autonomy was impracticable, and that full and complete union alone would meet the needs of the two countries. Eritrea's dependence on Ethiopian charity may seem to justify this attitude in the past and to provide sufficient excuse for Ethiopia if she should

[18] In 1952 there were in Eritrea 100 primary schools with 13,500 pupils, 14 middle schools with 1,200 pupils, and 2 secondary schools with 167 pupils. Thirty students were receiving higher education abroad.

Eritrea

now exploit her position as patron to bring about the union she has always demanded. That she might be tempted to do so is understandable. With an Ethiopian Governor General and an Ethiopian garrison in the territory, with Ethiopian control of the broadcasting services, and with Eritrea dependent on Ethiopian financial aid, she has the means of paralysing any Eritrean Government and of putting an end to any semblance of Eritrean autonomy. She would, however, be ill-advised to do so. As senior partner in the Federation, Ethiopia has a right to expect Eritrea to follow her leadership loyally; in return for financial and other aid she has a right to expect Eritrea to listen to her advice and be considerate of her interests. What she cannot legitimately demand or expect is Eritrean subservience.

The Eritrean Moslem accepted a federal association with Ethiopia reluctantly; and he would be the first to resent undue Ethiopian control over his affairs. In such an event Ethiopia would do well to reflect on the changing Middle Eastern scene and the growing political influence and appeal of Islam. With British authority withdrawn from the Sudan, with British influence removed from Egypt, and with an independent Somalia already in sight, Ethiopia is becoming encompassed by ambitious, vigorous, and free Moslem states. In such circumstances Moslem discontent in Eritrea would be singularly dangerous. The Moslem leaders in Eritrea came to learn the political value of their Islamic connexions during the latter part of the Occupation. If they have reason for discontent in the future they will undoubtedly exploit them. Should they do so, their appeals are likely to command Moslem sympathy, entailing the threat of active subversion and encouragement to revolt, not only among the Moslems of Eritrea but among the very much larger Moslem population of Ethiopia as well.

Undue Ethiopian interference in Eritrean affairs might also provoke a dangerous, if not immediate, reaction on the part of the Eritrean Abyssinians. Because the Unionist Party accepted Ethiopian instructions when it depended on Ethiopian support, it should not be supposed that the Unionists of yesterday will dance as happily to Ethiopian tunes tomorrow. The significance of the development of political consciousness among the Eritrean Abyssinians was not that they had demanded union with Ethiopia but that many had learned how to think for themselves and to express what they thought. Union with Ethiopia had an emotional appeal for them; but, fundamentally, the reason why they supported the Unionist Party was that they believed their interests would be better served under Ethiopian than under European colonial rule. Should there be discontent on the Eritrean Plateau it is likely to be echoed in the

The Transition to Autonomy, 1951–2

Tigrai and to revive dreams of an Eritrean-Tigrinyan union. Ethiopia would be unwise to risk such an eventuality.

It is for Ethiopia to make her choice. The temptation to subject Eritrea firmly under her own control will always be great. Should she try to do so, she will risk Eritrean discontent and eventual revolt, which, with foreign sympathy and support, might well disrupt both Eritrea and Ethiopia herself. Though an autonomous Eritrea has admittedly unwelcome implications for Ethiopia, her need for a loyal and stable Eritrea far transcends any inconvenience a federal relationship may impose upon her. It is to her own interest as well as to Eritrea's that she should ensure that the Federation survives in the form its authors intended. The future of the Federation, and indeed of the whole group of young countries in North East Africa, is likely to be affected by the course that Ethiopia takes. She has acquired a great responsibility.

APPENDIX

POPULATION OF ERITREA: COMMUNAL AND RELIGIOUS GROUPINGS[1]

	Christian[2]	Moslem	Pagan	Total
(i) Tigrinyans				
Hamasain.	117,000	1,000	—	118,000
Serai.	161,000	7,000	—	168,000
Akelli Guzai.	108,000	1,000	—	109,000
Urban and others.	101,000	28,000	—	129,000
	487,000	37,000	—	524,000
(ii) Tigray				
Bani Amir.	—	80,000	—	80,000
Sahel tribes.[3]	—	114,000	—	114,000
Maria.	—	43,000	—	43,000
Mensa.	7,000	4,000	—	11,000
Bait Juk.	—	4,000	—	4,000
Samhar.	—	35,000	—	35,000
Urban and others.	—	42,000	—	42,000
	7,000	322,000	—	329,000
(iii) Baria and Kunama				
Baria.	—	15,000	—	15,000
Kunama.	3,000	12,000	7,000	22,000
Urban and others.	—	4,000	—	4,000
	3,000	31,000	7,000	41,000
(iv) Danakil				
North Danakil.	—	23,000	—	23,000
South Danakil.	—	5,000	—	5,000
Urban and others.	—	5,000	—	5,000
	—	33,000	—	33,000

[1] The figures given are, to the nearest thousand in each case, those of the British Administration in 1952. They are based on returns by village heads and the leaders of tribal sections. They may be regarded as approximate.

[2] It should be noted that the 'Christian' population includes 459,000 Coptic Christians, 35,000 Roman Catholics (according to the Ethiopian rite), and 16,000 Protestants of the Swedish Evangelical Church.

[3] 'Sahel tribes' is the collective name adopted by the tribes which evolved after the break up of the Bait Asgaday and the Ad Shaikh (a tribe whose dominant family came from the Sudan in the nineteenth century).

Appendix

	Christian	Moslem	Pagan	Totals
(v) *Saho*				
Assa'orta.	—	35,000	—	35,000
Minaferi.	—	19,000	—	19,000
Hazu.	1,000	6,000	—	7,000
Debrimaila.	1,000	1,000	—	2,000
Sana'fay.	—	1,000	—	1,000
Urban and others.	—	2,000	—	2,000
	2,000	64,000	—	66,000
(vi) *Belain*				
Bait Tarqay	10,000	7,000	—	17,000
Bait Tauqay	—	19,000	—	19,000
Urban and others.	1,000	1,000	—	2,000
	11,000	27,000	—	38,000
Total:[4]	510,000	514,000	7,000	1,031,000

[4] In addition to the Eritrean population there were, in 1952, 17,000 Europeans (mostly Italians), 10,000 Arabs, and about 6,000 Sudanese, Somalis, and West Africans. The total population of Eritrea is accordingly about 1,064,000, of whom 32,000 are aliens.

INDEX

ABRAHA TESEMMA, DEJAZMATCH, 62, 98
Abraham, Abuna, 60 n.
Abyssinia, *see* Ethiopia
Abyssinians, 11 n.; connexion with Eritrea, 4 ff., 13 ff. *See also* Christian Abyssinians
Ad Taklais, the, 14 n., 71
Ad Temariam, the, 14 n.
Administrative divisions, 26
Adowa, battle of, 9
Adulis (Zula), 5
'Agau, the, 6, 11, 15
Agriculture, 39–40, 53
Akelli Guzai, the, 11, 26, 62, 69, 90, 96, 109, 132
Aklilu, Ato, 116 f.
'Ali Muhammad Idris ('Ali Muntaz), 70–71, 105
Anze Matienzo, Sr. Eduardo, 101, 103, 111 ff., 122
Arabia, South, 4 f.
Arabic language, 34, 78, 116 f., 121, 124
Arabs, 46 f., 50–51, 61, 66 f., 133
Asmara, 22, 34, 128; disturbances in, 67–68, 96; economic development, 36 ff., 40; elections, 118 ff.; growth and social structure, 46; importance for Ethiopia, 58; local administration, 27, 30, 51–52
Assab, 8, 26, 41, 46, 70, 85, 90
Assa'orta, the, 15, 55, 133
Aung Khine, 99 ff.
Aussa, Sultans of, 6, 14, 74
Axum, city, 63; Kingdom of, 4–5

BAHRI, THE, 1, 4, 59
Bait Asgaday, the, 14, 132 n.
Bait Juk, the, 14 n., 132
Bait Tarqay, the, 15–16, 133
Bait Tauqay, the, 15–16, 133
Bani Amir, the, 14, 55, 70–71, 75, 83, 97, 105, 109, 132
Banks, 43, 45
Baraka, River, 1, 3
Baraka Lowlands, 3 ff., 13 f., 21, 39 f., 58, 70–71. *See also* Bani Amir
Baria, the, 16, 58, 71, 73 f., 132
Beja tribes, 5 f., 13
Belain, the, 15–16, 80, 95, 133
Benoy, Brig. J. M., 69, 113 n.
Bevin, Ernest, 93
Bitwoded Andargachew, 75
Bogus, 15

British Administration: achievements of, 35–36, 128; establishment of, 18–24; proposed continuation of, 65 f., 74 f., 81, 100; relief and reconstruction, 22; social and political reforms, 29 ff., 35; system of government, 24–29; transfer of power, 121–8; transition period, 101, 103
British forces, entry of, 18
Budget, 43–45, 126
Burin des Roziers, Étienne, 86
Byrnes, James F., 85

CHRISTIAN ABYSSINIANS: attitude of to British, 51–52, 57, 61–62, —to Italians, 49 ff., 61; during Italian regime, 46–47, 52; and future of Eritrea, 82, 88 ff.; grievances of, in country, 52–57; —in towns, 47–52; numbers and distribution of, 11, 132–3; social status, 46. *See also* Coptic Church; Nationalist movement; Shifta; Tigrinyans; Unionist Party; *and under* Moslems
Christians, 11, 13, 15 ff., 132–3. *See also* Christian Abyssinians, Coptic Church; *and under* Moslems
Citizenship and electoral rights, 119
Civil service, 123–6. *See also* British Administration; Officials
Climate, 1–4
Coastal Plain: described, 1, 3 f., 39; Ethiopian claim to, 58; historical background, 4, 6 ff.; population, 13 ff. *See also* Danakil
Communications, 36, 127
Constitution, 113 ff., 126 ff.; terms of, 120–1, 122–3
Coptic Church, 6, 13, 58, 59–60, 96, 100
Cost of living, 47
Cumming, Sir Duncan, 113
Cyrenaica, 19, 84 f., 93

DANAKIL, THE, DANKALIA, 6, 8, 14, 58, 74 f., 80, 90, 98, 109, 132
Dawit Ogbazghi, Ato, 65
Debrimaila, the, 15, 133
Democratic Bloc, 114 ff., 119 f.
Di Gropello, Count, 95
Drew, Brig. F. G., 113 n.

ECONOMIC DEVELOPMENT, 36–43; British policy, 37 ff., 44–45; during war, 37–

134

Index

38, 42, 47 f.; Italian policy, 36–37, 39 ff.; natural resources, 38–41; supply organization, 42; viability, 81–82, 98 ff., 129. *See also* Foreign Trade
Eden, Sir Anthony, 85
Education, 33–34, 47, 78, 129
Egypt, Egyptians, 7–8, 16
Elections, 88–89, 118–20
Eritrea, disposal of after war, 57, 66, 68 f., 83 ff.; Bevin–Sforza Agreement, 93; consequences of delay, 92, 102; four-Power negotiations, 83–86, 90 ff. *See also* Ethiopia: Union with; Federation; Four Power Commission; Independence; Partition; United Nations
Eritrean Advisory Councils, 32–33
Ethiopia: access to sea, 85, 90; administration by proposed, 90; autonomy within, 74; British assurances to, alleged, 58–59; ecoonmic links with Eritrea, 36, 43 ff., 58, 82; effects of intervention by, 102; Eritrean indifference towards, 59; Italy and (1885–98), 9; —invasion and conquest (1935–6), 9–10; strategic importance of Eritrea for, 58; union of Eritrea with, 57 ff., 74 f., 78, 81, 88 ff., 100 f.; —pros and cons of, 82. *See also*: Abyssinians; Federation; Nationalist movement; Partition; Tigrai; Unionist Party; *and under* Shifta
Ethiopia-Hamasain Society, 65–66
Exports, 36 ff.

Fascism, 22 f., 77–78
Federation (with Ethiopia), 83, 98, 100 f.; 113 ff.; federal and other services, 127; inauguration of, 127–8; prospects of, 128–31. *See also* Constitution
Feodorov, A. F., 86
Finance, 43–45
Fisheries, 41
Flag, 116 f., 121
Foreign trade, 36, 42–43. *See also* Exports; Imports
Forestry, 40–41
Four Power Commission, 86–90, 91 f.
France, 83 ff., 90
Fung, the, 6 f., 14

Garcia Bauer, Carlos, 99 f.
Gash, River, 1, 3
Gash-Setit Lowlands, 3 f., 21, 39 ff.; fighting in, 70 f., 105, 109; historical background, 4, 6 f., 10; population, 16, 132
Gebremaskal Woldu, 60–61, 74
Ge'ez language, 5, 13

Gold, 41–42
Gordon, General, 8
Great Britain; and future of Eritrea, 58 f., 64, 69–70, 83 ff., 90; and other Italian colonies, 83 ff.; policy in 19th century, 7 f. *See also* British Administration
Gugsa, Haile Selassie, 63

Habab, the, 14 n.
Habash, the, 4–5
Hadendowa, the, 70–71, 75, 83, 97, 105
Haile Mariam, Blatta, 63 f.
Haile Selassie, Emperor, 58 f., 63, 127
Hamasain, the, 11, 26, 65 f., 109, 312
Hamitic peoples, 4 ff., 14 f.
Hazu, the, 15, 133
Health services, 34–35
Himyarites, 5, 13
Historical background, 4–11

Imports, 42 f.; from Italy, 37, 39 f.
Independence, 75, 81, 99 ff.; Italian support for, 93 ff.; not practicable, 81–82
Independence Bloc, 94 ff. *See also* Democratic Bloc
Industry, 37–38, 42
Italian Peace Treaty (1947), 68 f., 83, 92
Italian regime: acquisition of colony, 8; economic policy, 36–37, 39 ff.; Eritreans, in Italian army, 104–5; —treatment of, 29, 46–47; land question, 53–54; maintenance of order, 104; merits and demerits of rule, 11–12; taxation, 56
Italians, 18–19, 21 ff., 47, 76–78; attacks on, 55, 68, 91, 96, 109 f., 112; British policy towards, 21 ff., 30, 77 ff.; Eritrean hostility to, 49–50, 53–55, 57, 65 ff.; and future of Eritrea, 78, 90, 100; internment of, 23, 42, 76; number of, 22, 133; ownership of land, 53–54; repatriation of, 42. *See also under* Officials
Italo-Eritrean Association, 93–94
Italo-Eritreans, 50, 93, 119
Italy: agreement on educational and health services, 126; disposal of other colonies, 83–86, 93, 95; and future of Eritrea, 78–80, 92 ff., 102; pro-Italian feeling, 74 f., 79 f., 82. *See also under* Officials; Trusteeship

Jennings, Sir Ivor, 117
Jiberti, 13, 46 f., 70, 73 ff., 80, 82; hostility to, 13, 50–51, 55–56, 61
John IV, Emperor, 7 ff., 63

Index

KENNEDY-COOKE, Brig. B., 21 f., 24
Keren, 7 f., 15, 18 f., 26, 46, 80
Khatmia sect, 13, 74
Klimov, Mr., 87
Kunama, the, 16, 58, 74 f., 105, 109, 132

LAND TENURE, 11, 52–55, 56 f.; Church estates, 59
Language question, 33 f., 116 f., 121. *See also* Arabic; Tigrinya
Law and the Judiciary, 27–28, 31, 50, 52, 56, 122–3, 126
Liberal Progressive Party, 75 f., 81, 94, 97–98. *See also* Independence Bloc
Liberal Unionist Party, 98, 116
Libya, 84–85, 93, 95
Lira, devaluation of, 45
Livestock, 38–39
Longrigg, Brig. S. H., 35–36, 64, 69–70, 128

MAHABER FEKRI HAGER, 60–61
Mangasha, Ras, 9
Mareb, River, *see* Gash
Maria, the, 14, 132
Marqos, Abuna, 60, 64 f.
Massawa, 6 ff., 18, 37, 41, 58, 69, 82; administrative division, 26; attitude of Moslems, 70, 74, 80, 120; elections, 118 ff.; municipality, 27; railway and ropeway, 36, 127
Massawa, Na'ibs of, 70, 73
Menelik, Emperor, 8–9, 63
Mensa, the, 14, 132
Minaferi, the, 15, 133
Minerals, 41–42
al-Mirghani, Sayid Bubakr bin Othman, 74
Molotov, V. M., 85
Moslem League, 74 ff., 78 ff., 94 f., 97 f.; extent of support for, 88 f.; of Western Province, 97–98, 116 f., 120. *See also* Independence Bloc
Moslems, attacks on, 76, 91, 96, 109; Christian hostility to, 13, 50 ff., 55–56, 61, 76, 129; Christian-Moslem clashes, 96, 109; distribution of, 13 ff.; and future of Eritrea, 70, 73 ff., 81 ff., 88 ff., 90, 94 f., 97 f., 116 f., 120; law, 27 f., 123; pro-Italian feeling among, 74 f., 78; prospects of under federation, 129 f. *See also* Arabs; Jiberti; Tigray tribes
Municipalities, 27
Munzinger, Werner, 7

NATIONALIST MOVEMENT, 59–69; Ethiopian support for, 65 f.; and Separatists, 62 ff. *See also* Unionist Party
National unity, absence of, 4, 10–11, 129
Native administration, 11, 13 ff., 31–33, 56. *See also* Social and tribal structure
Newbold, Sir Douglas, 69
Nilotic peoples, 4, 6, 16. *See also* Baria, Kunama
Northern Highlands, 1, 3 f.; Ethiopian claim to, 57; historical background, 4 ff.; population, 13 ff., 132 f.; products, 39 f. *See also* Tigray tribes

OFFICIALS: British, 35–36, 51, 125 f., 128; Eritrean, 45, 47–48, 64; Eritreanization, 26, 30–31, 124–6; Italian, 21, 26, 30, 45, 49 ff., 77, 124 ff.

PANKHURST, Miss Sylvia, 66, 91
Partition, 69–70, 75, 78, 82 ff., 90, 93, 97 f., 100, 117; pros and cons, 82–83
Plateau, 1, 4; Ethiopian claim to, 57 f.; historical background, 4 ff.; natural resources, 39 ff.; support for union with Ethiopia, 89. *See also* Christian Abyssinians; Tigrinyans
Platt, Sir W., 18 f., 21
Police, 21, 26, 31, 49, 51 f., 105–6, 125; strike, 64–65
Political consciousness, growth of, 29, 46 ff., 52, 128
Population, 11–17, 132–3; European, 36, 42, 133 n.; urban, 46
Pro-Italy Party, 79–80, 89, 93 f., 98

QERILLOS, ABUNA, 60 n.
Qvale, Erling, 99 f.

RACIAL LAWS, 30, 50
Racial and religious groups, 11–17, 46, 132–3
Radai, Shaikh 'Ali Musa, 97
Rainfall, 3–4, 39
Rijpperda Wierdsma, Dr. 117

SABAEANS, 4–5, 13
Sahel tribes, 132
Saho tribes, 14 f., 55, 69, 73 ff., 80, 89, 98, 109, 120, 133
Samhar, the, 69 f., 73, 75, 98
Sana'fay, the, 15, 133
Separatists, 62 ff., 73 ff. *See also* Liberal Progressive Party
Serai, the, 11, 26, 90, 109, 132
Setit, River, 3. *See also* Gash-Setit Lowlands
Seyum, Ras, 63, 75

Index

Sforza, Count, 93
Shifta, 91–92, 96, 103 ff.; Ethiopian support for, 91–92, 105 ff.
Social and tribal structure, 11, 13 ff., 46, 52–53, 71–73
Social welfare, 22, 34 f.
Somalia, 84 f., 93, 95
Stafford, F. E., 86
Sudan, proposal to incorporate Moslem areas in, 69–70, 83, 93, 97 f., 120
Sudanese, 51, 61, 67 f. *See also* Hadendowa
Sultan, Ibrahim, 72 ff., 94, 97 f., 115, 120

Takazze, River, *see* Setit
Taxation, 35, 44 f., 56–57
Tedla Bairu, Ato, 69
Tenange Worq, Princess, 75
Tesemma Asberom, Ras, 62 f., 65
Theron, Maj. Gen. F. H., 99 ff.
Tigrai, the, 6 f., 9, 53, 63 f.; suggested union with Eritrea, 65, 97, 131
Tigray tribes, 13–14, 57 f., 70, 96, 109; and future of Eritrea, 74 f., 82 f., 97 f.; serfs emancipated, 17–73
Tigrinya language, 13, 33 f., 78, 116 f., 121, 124
Tigrinyans, 9, 11, 13, 58, 132. *See also* Christian Abyssinians; Tigrai
Tripolitania, 84–85, 93. *See also* Libya
Trusteeship, 75, 78, 81, 84–85, 93 f.; British, 75, 81, 84, 90, 94; collective, 85, 90, 100; Italian, 79, 81–82, 84 f., 90, 93 f.; for other Italian colonies, 84–85, 93, 95
Turkish rule, 6 f.

Uccialli, Treaty of, 9
Union of Soviet Socialist Republics, 83 ff., 90–91
Unionist Party, 69, 74 f., 79, 88, 92, 95 ff., 116 ff., 130; extent of support for, 88 f., 120; and Shifta, 92, 96, 106 ff., 110 f., 113
United Nations: Commission, 95, 98–101; Commissioner, *see* Anze Matienzo, Sr.; General Assembly, 83, 91 ff., 95; —resolution (2 Dec. 1950), 101; —resolution (29 Jan. 1952), 126 n. *See also* Trusteeship
United States of America, 37, 83, 85 f., 88 ff.
Unrest and terrorism, 67–68, 70–71, 91–92, 96, 102, 103-15; countermeasures, 105 ff., 110–13. *See also* Shifta; *and under* Italians; Moslems
Utter, J. E., 86

Van Biljoen, Dr. F., 100

Woldeab Woldemariam, Ato, 65, 115

Zagwe Dynasty, 6
Zaud Din, Mian, 99 f.
Zula, 5